BATTLEFIELD RATIONS

"An Army marches on its stomach", observed Napoleon; a hundred and fifty years later General Rommel remarked that the British should always be attacked before soldiers had had an early morning cup of tea. This book, written to raise money for the Army Benevolent Fund and with a Foreword by General Lord Dannatt, sets out the human story of the food and "brew-ups" of the front-line soldier from the Boer War to Helmand. Throughout, the importance of the provision of food, or even a simple mug of tea, for morale and unit fellowship as well as for the need of the calories required for battle is highlighted with many examples over the century. For many, until 1942, the basis of food was "bully beef" and hard biscuit, supplemented by whatever could be found locally, all adequate but monotonous. Sometimes supply failed, on occasions water also. The extremes of hardship being when regiments were besieged, as in Ladysmith in the Boer War and Kut El Amara in Iraq in the 1914-18 war. At Kut soldiers had, at best, hedgehogs or birds fried in axle-grease with local vegetation. On the Western Front the Retreat from Mons in August 1914 was almost as severe. The transport of food is as interesting a story as the food itself, ranging from oxen, horses, mules, camels, even reindeer and elephants to motor transport and aircraft in different theatres at different times. The first airdrop of food, not very successful, was in fact at Kut El Amara in 1916. The inter-war years experiences of mountaineers and polar explorers, supplemented by academic diet studies of the unemployed in London and North England led to the introduction of the varied composite, or 'compo' rations, marking an enormous improvement in soldiers' food, an improvement commented upon by the bully beef and biscuits-fed 8th Army advancing into Tunisia from Libya on meeting the 1st Army which had landed in Algeria with tins of compo. The Italian campaigns of 1943-45, especially the Salerno and Anzio landings and the battle for Monte Cassino, presented particular difficulties. At Cassino food reached forward units on mules with Basuto muleteers and Indian porters for the last stage to men in ground holes or scrapes. Soldiers landing in Normandy and fighting on into Germany were generally well fed even during a hard 1944-45 winter. The worst suffering, though, fell on soldiers in the Burma campaign, especially in the Chindit columns. In one unit the only food available at one time was the chaplain's store of Communion wafers. Many men died unnecessarily from the results of poor feeding.

In the end of empire colonial campaigns soldiers were generally well fed even if the food was monotonous. Units in the Korean War experienced difficulties at the onset; in the Borneo jungle campaigns of the 1960s the problem was not so much the provision of food for patrols as how to eat it without the smell of the food and refuse from the packs giving positions away. For the Falklands War special cold weather compo had to be provided and was eaten on the long 'yomps', 'tabs', or marches. The soldier on the streets of Northern Ireland often lived on egg "banjo" sandwiches but real hardship was suffered by one Welsh battalion besieged by the Serbs in Gorazde during the Bosnia operations when Vitamin C deficiency led to scurvy. The book ends with food supply, often based on whole or part-swapping with American military food (usually below British standards) in the Iraq operations and in Afghanistan.

An appendix sets out the contents of a typical box of rations issued to a soldier in Helmand in 2011, very generous in quantity and easily prepared. One side of the box carries a stern message to the effect that a soldier must consume the entire contents in order to maintain full fighting efficiency. Such injunctions were not marked on the boxes of food sent forward to the troops in the Boer War; there the boxes were stamped with the initials of the Senior Catering Office Field Force, hence "Scoffs here at last."

The work has been compiled from documents in the Royal Logistic Corps Museum at Deepcut, from memoirs, letters and interviews, and from the superb collection of regimental histories in the library of the Royal Military Academy Sandhurst.

All royalties due to the author for this book will be sent to the Army Benevolent Fund, The Soldiers' Charity.

Dr Anthony Clayton was a lecturer at the Royal Military Academy Sandhurst from 1965 to 1993 and an Associate Lecturer at the University of Surrey from 1994 to 2008. A graduate of the University of St Andrews, he served in the colonial government of Kenya until 1963; he also served in the Territorial Army in the infantry and the Intelligence Corps, finishing as a lieutenant-colonel. His published works include books on British and French military history, among them *The British Empire As A Superpower 1919-1939* and *The British Officer from 1660 to the Present*, together with *France, Soldiers and Africa, The Wars of French Decolonization* and *Paths of Glory, the French Army 1914-1918*. For his work on the French Army he was made a Chevalier dans l'Ordre des Palmes Académiques. He contributed chapters to several other works including *Dresden, A City Reborn*, Volume 4 of the *Oxford History of the British Empire* and the *Cambridge History of War. Warfare in Woods and Forests* was published in 2011. *Battlefield Rations*, he hoped, will make a useful contribution to the Army Benevolent Fund to which all royalties due to him are to go. Typing of the manuscript was also a voluntary contribution from a former Surrey University colleague, Gillian James, and the author was greatly indebted to General Lord Dannatt for his kind foreword. Anthony Clayton died in 2021.

BATTLEFIELD RATIONS

THE FOOD GIVEN TO THE BRITISH SOLDIER FOR MARCHING AND FIGHTING 1900-2011

Anthony Clayton

Helion & Company

Helion & Company Limited
Unit 8 Amherst Business Centre
Budbrooke Road
Warwick
CV34 5WE
England
Tel. 01926 499 619
Email: info@helion.co.uk
Website: www.helion.co.uk
X: @helionbooks
Visit our blog https://helionbooks.wordpress.com/

Published by Helion & Company 2013
Designed and typeset by Aspect Book Design (www.aspectbookdesign.com)
Cover designed by Paul Hewitt, Battlefield Design (www.battlefield-design.co.uk)

Text © Anthony Clayton 2013
Images © as individually credited

Front cover: 'Lull in the Battle' – soldiers of the Army Catering Corps providing hot food and tea to soldiers of the 2nd Battalion the Parachute Regiment, Falklands War 1982, by Terence Cuneo, courtesy of The Royal Logistic Corps Association Trust.

ISBN 978 1 909384 18 7

British Library Cataloguing-in-Publication Data.
A catalogue record for this book is available from the British Library.

All rights reserved. No part of this publication may be reproduced, stored in a retrieval system, or transmitted, in any form, or by any means, electronic, mechanical, photocopying, recording or otherwise, without the express written consent of Helion & Company Limited.

For details of other military history titles published by Helion & Company Limited contact the above address, or visit our website: http://www.helion.co.uk.

We always welcome receiving book proposals from prospective authors.

Contents

List of Illustrations	viii
Foreword	ix
Introduction	xi
The Boer War: 1899–1902	13
The First World War: The Western Front 1914–1918	20
The First World War: Other Theatres 1914–1918	29
The Inter-War Years: 1919–1939	40
The Second World War: 1939–1942	43
The Second World War: 1942–1945	55
The Post-War Years 1945–1965	70
The Post-War Years: 1968–2010	83
Conclusion	97
Appendix	99
Sources & Select Bibliography	101
Index	112

List of Illustrations

The British Army biscuit, Boer War.	16
British Army emergency ration pack, Boer War.	17
A field oven during the Boer War.	18
A cavalry squadron mess cart.	19
The all-important cup of tea.	21
A company-level field kitchen, 1915.	24
Arrival of the bread ration for a company of the Gloucestershire Regiment.	24
A British Army field kitchen, c 1917.	25
WAAC cooks at work at Camp No.1, Abbeville, 1917.	26
'The Anzac Walk'.	31
Camel supply, Palestine Campaign, 1918.	35
A field bakery using the Aldershot Oven, Salonika, 1915.	36
Territorial Army training on a No 1 Cooker, 1939.	41
Soldiers of the British Expeditionary Force in France drawing food from a protected field kitchen, 1939.	44
Siege of Malta.	48
A British tank crew having a 'brew up' in North Africa, c 1941.	49
Loading valuable food supplies onto trucks during the retreat from Libya.	52
A soldier of the Green Howards eating a salmon sandwich outside his Anzio beachhead dug-out.	58
Soldiers of 107 Regiment Royal Armoured Corps.	61
A Chindit and mule.	66
Rations issued in Malaya to an infantry battalion.	72
The Regimental Sergeant Major of an artillery regiment turning his hand at cooking.	77
A party given by an artillery regiment for Korean children.	79
Soldier of the 3rd Battalion the Parachute Regiment eating dinner.	85
A soldier of the Royal Scots Dragoon Guards has an American MRE meal during the Gulf War, February 1991.	87
Mules can replenish those places to which motor vehicles cannot travel.	89
An officer of 13 Company, 15 (Airborne) Signals Regiment, cooking a meal.	94

Foreword

While every schoolboy has heard it said that "an army marches on its stomach", it takes those who have served as soldiers to know that this is true. Ammunition for the guns, diesel for the vehicles and mail from home – all these things are vital to military operations – but good food is the key ingredient to high morale, and high morale is what makes soldiers fight hard and armies win. When Napoleon Bonaparte coined that well-known dictum about an army marching on its stomach, he also said that "the moral is to the physical, as three is to one". By this he meant that an army, in his day, might be equipped with the best "physical" things - cannons, muskets and the finest uniforms - but if their will to win – the "moral" aspect was lacking, then their chances of success on the battlefield were poor. In this well thought out book Anthony Clayton has underlined once more the importance of what Napoleon Bonaparte knew to be true – it is morale that matters more than kit. In "Battlefield Rations" Anthony Clayton sets out a compelling case to substantiate the importance of food to the soldier, and the place of food, or "scoff" as it is known to soldiers, in military history.

Why "scoff"? Like most things military, there is logic involved and invariably an acronym. Food first became known as "scoff" in the Boer War when ration packs sent forward to units in the field were stamped with the abbreviated title of the **S**enior **C**atering **O**fficer **F**ield **F**orce, thus the word SCOFF entered the military lexicon. For soldiers who have taken part in overseas operations in recent times, in places like Bosnia, Kosovo, Iraq and Afghanistan, there is no doubt that good "scoff" remains an essential ingredient of military success.

With his clever examination of the Army Catering Corps' archives at Deepcut and the rich collection of material lodged in the library of the Royal Military Academy Sandhurst, augmented by extracts from letters and interviews with both serving soldiers and veterans, Anthony Clayton has put together a fascinating account of the role of food on the battlefield. He describes not only how food was cooked, but how it was moved from kitchen to mess tin, and how it was received on the front line. From "bully beef" to "compo" and from "Benghazi Burners" to "Hexy Cookers", the culinary journey to Tommy Atkins' stomach is traced in an authentic and amusing way.

Front line soldiers have traditionally given their chefs something of a hard time, but behind the banter there is a deep affection for those who produce remarkable food in the worst of conditions, at all hours. Some worry today, that the trend towards civilian 'contractorisation' and out-sourcing of cooking will erode the quality of military chefs and undermine their battle-winning status. This is a risk that will need to be watched and managed carefully in the cash-strapped years ahead, but any policymaker that doubted the importance of chefs in uniform must certainly sit down with a copy of this book. We tinker with the scoff, and the men and women who produce it at our peril. This most entertaining of books will give great pleasure, enlightenment and sustenance to the military enthusiast and general reader alike. Anthony Clayton has served up a menu that provides for all tastes, and will have the diners looking for more.

Richard Dannatt

General the Lord Dannatt GCB CBE MC DL
Chief of the General Staff 2006-2009
Constable of HM Tower of London

Introduction

I wrote this book with the hope and the purpose that it might raise money for the Army Benevolent Fund. At the time of writing the conflict in Afghanistan was and still is costing soldiers' lives, with many others returning home shattered by disabling physical and psychological injuries. There can be no more deserving charity that one helping these victims and their families.

As this book took shape I became aware that it might also claim to fill a niche in twentieth century British Army history, showing readers the front line soldier's very basic need for food, even if only the all important cup of tea, to keep going amid the horrors and fears of the battlefield. A second purpose accordingly began to appear, important in the age of cost reductions of this time and that, unfortunately, it seems necessary to emphasise. Reductions in the quality of food for soldiers in combat, or earlier in training for some financially expedient reason is neither fair for the soldier nor conducive to military efficiency. Political and military leaders and officials on both sides of the road in Whitehall must not regard food or the personnel concerned with its provision as an area for cost-cutting.

This work has of necessity to be limited to the most important twentieth and twenty-first century campaigns, with emphasis on the ordinary front-line soldier. Space cannot permit of a study of the many lesser operations and commitments, nor of the operations of special forces. The ordinary soldier is the mass of the Army; this work is about an important aspect of his life.

A number of people have helped me in producing this work, and it is a pleasure to acknowledge my debt of gratitude. In particular, there are several persons without whose help this work would simply never have appeared. The first of these is Mrs Gillian James who has patiently and thoroughly managed to decrypt my crab-style handwriting into type; this is no mean feat, and Gillian braved it freely as anxious as I to help the Army Benevolent Fund. John Card balanced my total lack of modern electronic communication with his own expertise, greatly facilitating research and the quest for photographs. Ned Willmott, an old and valued friend from the Sandhurst of the late 1960s onwards has helped me in a number of ways ranging from constructive criticism to help with transport to and from the Sandhurst Library. And also to a team, the Librarian of the Central Library of the Royal Military Academy Sandhurst, Andrew Orgill, and his assistants John Pearce and Ken Franklin for not only much help in locating source material for me but also enormously appreciated support and encouragement. Nothing ever seemed too much trouble for them, and Ken Franklin's ability to locate books that I needed before I could even unpack my briefcase ought to gain him an Olympic Medal.

Many others have contributed to the very wide field that this work covers and the material they have given me has added rich detail, so my thanks to Dr John Blair from whom I learnt the origin of the word 'Scoff', Flight Lieutenant M. Card, Dr C. Carlton, Lieutenant Colonel P.G. Duffield, Dr J.S.A, Edwards, Edgar Green of the Middlesex Korean Club, Major K. Grey of the Royal Green Jackets Museum, Julian James whose service with the Parachute Regiment included command in action of every rank from subaltern to battalion commander, Professor P. Jones, Brigadier 'Tank' Nash, Brigadier B.A.H. Parritt, Lieutenant-General Sir Hew Pike, David Read of the Gloucestershire Regiment Museum Andrew Robertshaw of the Royal Logistic Corps Museum and his archivist, Gareth Mears, Lieutenant-Colonel Edward Tremlett and Brigadier Henry Wilson.

As a book it proved enormously fascinating to write with numerous accounts of hardship, a few of horror, and many of that mixture unique to the British soldier, endurance of a grim often dangerous monotony spiced and relieved by humour and banter.

Anthony Clayton
Farnham, 2013

1

The Boer War: 1899–1902

A hot meal, or just the smell of cooking as a promise of food to come is a pleasure that we all enjoy. To a front line soldier amid the noise, fear and confusion of battle, the shock of friends wounded or dead in a foreign field, it is more than just enjoyment, particularly so if the soldier is alone, very much alone, in a small foxhole or scrape at night. A mess tin of hot tea has an effect out of all proportion to its size; and food along with friends from a unit cooker, even if tepid or cold, especially so. Even a simple brew of tea can provide a momentary return to the normal everyday world, a chance to talk and joke with comrades in group cohesion. Morale and determination are restored. Conversely, if the food is poor or after two or three days non-existent, morale fades away with the pangs of hunger. A wise commander will always ensure that it is not only the ammunition but also the rations, in particular tea, that are always sent up to the front.

The purpose of this small book is to tell readers what the British soldiers in actual combat with the enemy had been given to eat, either before or during battles over the last one hundred years. The food that actually reaches the soldier may not be quite the same as that set out in commanders' and staff ration scale directives. The full scale of rationing may not have been delivered in part, or sometimes not at all, as a consequence of changing events on the battlefield or muddles at staff levels; bad weather may have prevented wagon or vehicle movement; a long journey may have made some foodstuffs no longer fit to eat; civilians on the road may have filched some or all of the contents of a wagon or even other commanders; regiments or individuals may have yielded to a sudden temptation to help themselves. On the plus side regiments may have been able to supplement rations by local purchase, barter with civilians or soldiers of other armies by requisition or helping themselves from the local countryside. Soldiers in regiments in transit or in rest periods a mile or two behind the front line, could visit local small restaurants or grocers where these existed.

The most unfortunate in any war have been the wounded and soldiers taken prisoner by their enemy. Food necessary to support recovery and recuperation was not always to hand in the quantities needed. Prisoners held by the Turks in the First World War and the Japanese in the Second World War suffered severely. But theirs is another story, many accounts survive in other specialist works or memoirs.

Over the years big changes have greatly improved the front-line soldiers' food. First and perhaps most important of all has been the realisation by military authorities that proper food matters; the Boer War traditional tinned meat, hard biscuits and lemon juice just would not do, and also a recognition that the regiment or battalion cooking staff must be trained, no use simply putting the overweight and rather scruffy soldier that his officers did not know what to do with in the cook-house. At home in Britain the late nineteenth and early twentieth century developments in refrigeration and tinned foods and spirit-fuelled cookers enabled much better food to be provided, all other factors being equal. Similarly old ox and horse wagon transport has moved on to motor vehicles and air drops though that long suffering animal, the mule was still humping food loads in Italy as late as 1944 and Bosnia in 1995. The debt the army owes to animals, also in Rudyard Kipling's words "Her Majesty's Servants", to 'march and suffer' along with the men whose food they carried has never been fully appreciated. Composite, "compo", ration packs introduced from 1940 onwards for individuals or small groups or whole units seemed to banish poor feeding and transport problems forever until 1995, when a battalion besieged in a Bosnian town was reduced to fractions of formal rations and despite all modern progress scurvy actually reappeared.

Until the Crimean War of 1854-56 food for the soldier had been a matter of what was the least cost to the Treasury and taxpayer, what food contractors would provide when their profits counted for more than any thought of the well-being of soldiers, also just how much the soldier himself was prepared to put up with. Soldiers were expected to pay for their food by deductions from their meagre pay, though after 1873 bread or biscuits were supplied free. The meat when not fresh was 'bully beef', a term derived from the French *boeuf bouillé*, boiled beef. When tinned it was light and could be carried for long periods without serious deterioration, being without fat it was healthy and nourishing and easy to eat warmed up or cold if soldiers were very tired; it could also form the basis of stews. However, it could soon become monotonous, affecting soldiers' appetites day after day. In hot weather bully beef in tins increased thirst and was also liable to melt down into an unappetising very sticky mess. The quality could vary, soldiers became experts in judging the products of different manufacturers. On campaigns biscuits were considered preferable to bread, easier to keep clean and usable for a variety of other dishes if broken. The biscuits, in varying sizes and shapes, were generally very hard, creating problems for men with poor teeth. But, nevertheless, feeding for the British soldier was far from satisfactory and regiments went to South Africa in 1895 and 1899 with men poorly nourished and not very fit. In the infantry regiments, in peace composed of two battalions, one at home and one in India or Egypt, men were often recruited from the urban unemployed. In the regimental depots the best men had already been sent to the overseas battalion with the result that the home battalion hurriedly enlisted for South Africa had some of the least fit. Their need was a three-month period of good food and good training—they were given neither. Disease was to follow.

The official authorised rations for a soldier at the outbreak of the South African 'Boer' War was:

1¼ lb of bread or 1 lb of biscuits
¾ lb of preserved meat or 1 lb of fresh meat
3 ozs of sugar
4 ozs of jam
1/6 oz of pepper
2 ozs dried vegetables of if available fresh vegetables

For emergencies each soldier was to carry with him a one pound tin of prepared meat, one pound of biscuits and a packet containing small quantities of salt, sugar and tea.

Rations were to be prepared in boxes, each box marked with the stamp of the 'Senior Catering Officer Field Force' abbreviated to S.C.O.F.F. the abbreviation quickly becoming a word in the English language. The overall plan provided for food, stores and ammunition to be sent as far forward as the existing railway tracks could approach the combat zone, and then be moved forward in ox wagon columns of 100 wagons and 1,600 oxen, to supply parks. From there, when necessary, mules either pulling carts or carrying ration packs on their backs would take the food forward to units and outlying sub-units, companies and platoons. Each unit – regiment or battalion – was supposed to have sufficient transport for two days rations with oats for horses. A battalion (at that time formed of eight rifle companies) would have nine wagons allotted for it, one for each company and one for the headquarters. Bakers and butchers of the Army Service Corps were among logistic personnel sent out from Britain.

The British Army biscuit, Boer War. Crushed, it made good porridge. The photo shows a biscuit sent home from South Africa by Private Samuel Cooper, the King's Own Royal Regiment. (Regimental museum of the King's Own Royal Regiment)

Planning was however compromised by the sudden nature of the war and the absence of preparations, inept staff work by untrained and inexperienced officers, and difficulties in obtaining the huge numbers of oxen and mules. As the campaign developed with the need for battalions to have to march as much as thirty miles a day for several consecutive days the weight carried by wagons or individual soldiers on the march became a concern. The tinned meat often arrived in 14 pound tins, a heavy extra weight especially for the individual soldiers to carry, particularly if the weather was very hot. Many soldiers were tempted to open and eat the meat before the march began, leaving nothing for days to come, with nothing available on the march. Regiments were encouraged to buy provisions locally if available and rations were then greatly reduced.

Several other factors affected the supply columns. First, the climate. At different seasons of the year the weather could be days of sweltering heat or nights of bitter cold. Rain and thunderstorms could bring a supply column to a halt, weapons slipping off a track and coverings blown off. Boer strike attacks cut the railway lines and threatened the ox wagon columns. On the way local commanders would interfere, claiming that their local needs overrode the needs of the unit or supply park for which the rations were destined. A particularly unpleasant case was one where a major-general took over a whole battalion's worth of food for his staff and himself - less than twenty-five men. Occasionally soldiers, usually men who had suffered or were suffering from food shortage, resorted to pillaging.

Another unexpected difficulty was the 'biological clock' of the ox, prepared to work from 2 a.m. to 9 a.m. and again from 4 p.m. to 8 or 9 p.m. but wanting to graze or drink during much of the night. Attempts to make them work at other times or a night move simply led to their becoming unfit, many dying.

On operations soldiers food could be supplemented with fruit or vegetables when passing through a township where such foods were available, sometimes by purchase, sometimes by formal requisition and sometimes, particularly from Boer farmsteads, by simply taking what soldiers saw before them —milk, butter, poultry, pigs, ox meat, sheep, eggs, peaches, pears, pumpkins and other vegetables. On a few occasions tinned mutton replaced beef, a much welcome change. Later in the war one pound tins of 'Maconochie', a meat and vegetable stew which could be eaten hot or cold became available. Popular at first it was soon found to make soldiers liable to flatulence and over any long period jaundice. Quaker Oats, perhaps, also arrived. An important local addition used by almost all regiments was the local maize meal, eaten as a vegetable or ground down for porridge. Grinding machines were found and put to use. Cow dung and grass was used as fuel for cooking if wood was not to hand.

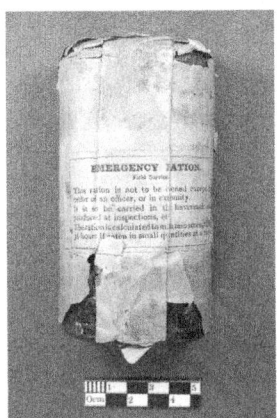

British Army emergency ration pack, Boer War. (Regimental museum of the King's Own Royal Regiment)

In actual campaigning the war fell into three phases, early reverses, a successful campaign ending formal Boer resistance and a Boer guerrilla campaign. The soldiers suffered most in the first part and early months of the second part, frequent long marches on half rations, combats in which for varying periods soldiers could only be fed on half rations or less, but in the final phase generally food was no longer short.

Regimental histories record detail. A battalion of the Buffs on a march noted "…half rations of bully beef, two biscuits, half a cup of tea with a tot of rum" as daily food; another battalion of Green Howards recorded a daily diet of five large biscuits and a pound of fresh trek ox. Bully beef was seen as a luxury. Some days units were without food or water in bitterly cold weather, or on half rations for over a month. At Spion Kop a West Yorkshire battalion had no fresh meat, bread or vegetables for nine days. Sometimes some of the official rations would arrive, but missing a vital component such as the biscuits, or the sugar or jam needed to make a palatable porridge out of crushed biscuits. In 1900 it was also apparent that soldiers in columns commanded by General Sir Redvers Buller were much better supplied with food than those in columns under General Lord Roberts who pushed his men for long periods on half rations or less.

A field oven during the Boer War. (Lieutenant Colonel J. Watkins-Yardley, *With the Iniskilling Dragoons. The Record of a Cavalry Regiment during the Boer War, 1899-1902*)

There does not appear to have been any ban on alcohol during the campaign. Regimental histories record purchases of beer from town stores on the march. On one occasion when the Devonshire Regiment had come to the rescue of a battalion of the Royal Dublin Fusiliers, the Irishmen rewarded every soldier of the Devons with a much appreciated tin of beer.

The regiments that suffered the worst were those cut off in the long early November 1899 – end of February 1900 siege of Ladysmith. The Gordon Highlanders history records that horse flesh from slaughtered horses had to form part of the menu in lieu of the meat ration and was generally disliked. Horse flesh was also used to make a pungent but not unpleasant soup called 'chevril'. Rations were reduced to one pound of meat, 'sausage of horse', four ounces of bread made from mealie meal and starch, and four ounces of maize meal itself or two and a half biscuits, the only vegetables the local wild spinach, and tea one sixth of an ounce. The maize meal was generally made into an acceptable porridge, a loaf or Indian chupatties and even a coffee substitute when burnt over embers. Dubbin was used as a cooking fat. Soldiers became weak from the lack of food. In the final weeks oxen were killed for their very tough meat known as 'T.O.', trek ox.

A cavalry squadron mess cart. (Lieutenant Colonel J. Watkins-Yardley, *With the Iniskilling Dragoons. The Record of a Cavalry Regiment during the Boer War, 1899-1902*)

The consequences were severe and well-known – disease, in particular dysentery and enteric fever, the latter usually caused by poisoned water. The Devonshire Regiment's 1st Battalion were reduced to men with 'shrunken stomachs, indigestion and jaundice' requiring two months good food supply to restore them to full fitness. Other battalions were in comparable conditions.

Although one of the Boer war's least successful generals, General Buller was nonetheless held in real affection by his soldiers for his known concern for their welfare. His biographer recounts the comment of an old soldier; "Now no one loves his dinner better than Buller, but if the canteen is not up Buller won't eat his dinner and when they 'ears that Buller can't eat his dinner they hurries up in the canteen and then Buller eats his dinner."

2

The First World War: The Western Front 1914–1918

The Western Front in the First World War was one of the worst experiences suffered by the British Army in its long history. In a line of trenches, summers and winters for four long years, soldiers were bombarded by German guns and mortars, attacked with poison gas and their trenches undermined by enemy engineers. They lived in mud, squalor, corpses, shell holes and rusty wire, infested by rats and lice; they were almost always short of sleep and longing for a wash and clean-up. They had doubts over the abilities of their generals to return them safely home to 'Blighty'. They lived each day in constant apprehension of what the morrow might bring, everyone aware of the huge casualties, most also saddened by the deaths of friends.

Food for the soldier in these conditions was a crucial factor in maintaining the fighting man's morale and combat efficiency. One of the most important lessons learnt from the Boer War experience was that of some understanding of the social and moral benefit when small groups of men could gather perhaps even huddle close together over a few items of warm food or even nothing more than a cup of warm tea.

In fact, a few other practical lessons and improvements had by 1914 been made in army feeding as a result of the Boer War experience. Several patterns of field kitchens, of varying sizes to meet varying needs of numbers of men, had been drawn up and instructions issued for their use. The pattern that fell into widest use was named, predictably, the 'Aldershot Kitchen', for troops likely to remain in the same location for two days or more. The kitchen was a construction of metal sections and bars to be erected above and around a dug trench, requiring wood fuel, but capable of cooking fifty-four two pound loaves of bread, or a meal for two hundred and twenty men all within four hours, second meal sittings taking about half that time. A number of suitable simple meat and soup recipes had been tested out. A school of cooking had been opened at a barracks in Aldershot, and also instructions revised to lay down that soldiers on the march should be given their food in small quantities with the main meal at the end of the day's march so as to avoid jaundice. Instructions issued also advised against suet and cabbage in the field.

In the event food supply on the Western Front can be summarised by saying that with the major exceptions of the war of movement periods of August to October 1914 and from July 1918 onwards, the height of the great offensives in 1915, the Somme in 1916, in 1917 the national food shortage caused by German submarine activity, and the great 'Third Ypres' offensives, the front line soldier was adequately fed when fighting was not immediate and intense, and particularly when units were in rest periods. The food may have been dreary, monotonous and unpalatable but it was edible and nourishing. For the soldier, during his service in the front line trenches and in attacks, food degraded to be generally horrible, and hot food could be non-existent for several days, with relaxation limited to a hot water brew of tea prepared in an old meat tin heated by a candle.

The all-important cup of tea. Men from the Argyll & Sutherland Highlanders in 1915, before the issue of the steel helmet. (Regimental museum of the Argyll & Sutherland Highlanders)

Wider factors had also helped the overall improvement from the SCOFF ration packs of the Boer War - improved refrigeration technology, some better understanding of the importance of vegetables, and the basic French railway system with wartime extensions together with, later, the growing number of petrol driven lorries. The first enabled the tinned meat less likely to deteriorate, the second a better balanced provision of food, especially including vitamins B and D, the third facilitated the distribution forward from ports to be much quicker. Also the water supply to units was generally, but not always to hand behind the lines; if not a supply would be brought up to the front in water tanks. The amount that actually reached the soldier varied and thirst could sometimes add to the soldier's discomfort. Water was often purified with chloride of lime giving it an unpleasant taste, even when boiled. From railheads and supply parks food supply remained transported by horse and wagon with a few exceptions such as in the Somme in 1916 and in Ypres in 1917 and the Marne in 1918 when mules and mule packs had to be used. For front-line units such as an infantry battalion (now four, no longer eight companies) there were four 'company cookers', a large kitchen with a collapsing chimney which was mounted on a limber pulled by two horses, the limber also carried the rations. Under a company sergeant cook were four cooks, available fatigue men would carry the boxes and make tea. Each company cooker had a large number of 'dixies', large cooking pots and the equipment needed to have a fire, if necessary above a dug-out trench. Food was prepared in fifty minutes from the cooker when assembled, but with the massive expansion of the wartime Army many of the cooks still lacked training or experience with often, in the words of one history the result was 'great goblets of fat floating in the enormous stew dixies'. In France brigades and divisions ran cooking courses but the field conditions prevented much real improvement beyond the occasional making of rissoles from bully beef, powdered biscuit and bacon fat or a boiled currant pudding from powdered biscuit and bacon drip for lard. The hay boxes were supposed to be made by up by units according to a pattern prescribed in an Army manual, double skinned; in practice many were improvised. By 1917 a felt lined light metal container had been manufactured. It was carried on the soldier's back leaving his arms and hands free, a big advantage for soldiers moving in narrow communication trenches. Overall the company cooker system worked well for static trench warfare, but in muddy or other difficult conditions was not sufficiently mobile. At least one unit converted oil drums into ovens for roasting meat by keeping a fire going under the drum.

The soldiers' 1914 official basic ration differed little from that of the Boer War, though an increase in the vegetable content was included. In 1917, however, for reasons of economy a distinction was drawn between soldiers in the front line and lines of communication personnel who drew a slightly lower scale. The normal higher rate, just over 4,000 – 4,200 calories, was:

Meat, fresh or frozen	1lb
Bacon	4 ozs
Bread	1lb or 10 ozs biscuits
Butter	2 ozs (three times per week)
Jam	3 ozs
Tea	⅝ oz
Sugar	3 ozs
Condensed Milk	1 oz
Oatmeal	3 ozs (three times a week)
Potatoes	2 ozs
Fresh vegetables	8 ozs (or 2 ozs dried vegetables)
Salt, pepper, mustard	

If available a portion of cheese and two cubes of meat extract were added but accounts suggest this was not always the case.

The intention was that the meat, usually bully beef, and the bread should be carried in large packs by the unit's wagons, available for cooking for a hot meal with any other food to hand. The soldier was to carry the tea, sugar and cheese for a light meal at other times. For emergencies or prior to a major assault soldiers would be given one or two days' worth of 'iron rations', a tin of bully beef and a tin of biscuits to add to his tea, sugar, cheese and meat cubes. In these circumstances the 'iron rations' would only be opened on the orders of an officer and eaten heated if possible, if not cold, from the soldiers' mess tins.

In the forward trenches, circumstances permitting, a variety of small trench or 'Tommy' cookers appeared as the war wore on, some were empty food tin heated by any solid fuel or paraffin or methylated spirits available. These could warm up ration food, make a hash of bully beef and crushed biscuit, or porridge from crushed biscuits and jam, if bread was available it could be toasted at the point of a bayonet, and if nothing else was available simply heat up a cup of tea from compressed tablets. They were however of little value in wind or heavy rain. Some soldiers arranged for primus stoves to be sent out from Britain. Other men acquired larger charcoal braziers or converted latrine buckets into braziers by punching holes in

A company-level field kitchen, 1915. (Regimental museum of the King's Own Royal Regiment)

Arrival of the bread ration for a company of the Gloucestershire Regiment. (Regimental museum of the Gloucestershire Regiment)

them with a bayonet, but their smoke made these a risk, identifiable by the enemy and anti-social in a dug-out. Fat for trench cooking was often a problem, Vaseline, Dubbin or rifle cleaning oil being used in desperation. But in front line dug-outs and trenches, food at best, was likely to be only Maconochie's stews, pork and beans or turnip and carrot in a watery gravy, acceptable when hot but very unappetising when cold, or a greasy stew made from bully beef, together with a chunk of far from fresh bread and the equally unappetising apple or quince jam. Sometimes, particularly in 1917 at the time of the serious shipping problem, a forward platoon or section's half rations were so much reduced to little or no bread, less than half a portion of meat and a spoonful of jam, that groups of men took it in day by day turns to eat the meagre portions. But this did not last long.

An important factor in keeping soldiers generally well-fed were the opportunities provided by unit rest periods. Soldiers could then visit local French small town or village *estaminets* and fill up with meat, bacon, omelettes, potatoes and vegetables, and then return to the front line with veal, sausages, bacon, tinned herrings or sardines, ham and fresh bread. The *estaminets* could also offer French dry white country wine and, much more popular Flemish-style beer. Occasionally the soldier's food could be supplemented by any captured German food. Regrettably, soldiers in some units were not above helping themselves to food that 'fell off the back of a wagon' of another unit. As the war progressed rations at different times and in different locations came to provide better quality porridge, condensed milk for use in porridge and in 'Army tea'; bacon fat into which men could dip bread, margarine, cheese and dried vegetables that arrived in sacks or even sandbags, and any local fresh vegetables or fruit. Packages of food from Britain also arrived in quantity, containing chocolate, fruit cake sometimes laced with brandy or rum, and sauce or curry powder to liven up the stews; tobacco was also often included.

A British Army field kitchen, c 1917. (National Library of Scotland)

With the approval of the area Division or Brigade commander a daily issue of lemon juice and much more important, up to one-sixth of a pint of rum could be authorised; in practice the amount usually given to a soldier was an egg cup-full. Most, but not all Division commanders duly authorised the rum issue, those who did not suffered a loss of morale in their formations. Some gave permission only in wet weather; rain apparently fell heavily on many battalions. The rum was extremely strong and had to be diluted in tea, and was issued either at early morning stand-to or in the evening. Two ounces of cigarettes or tobacco were issued free and nearly always available. The cigarettes could vary according to brand, Woodbines being the most popular. At that time no one was concerned, or even aware of, any health or reduced efficiency hazards.

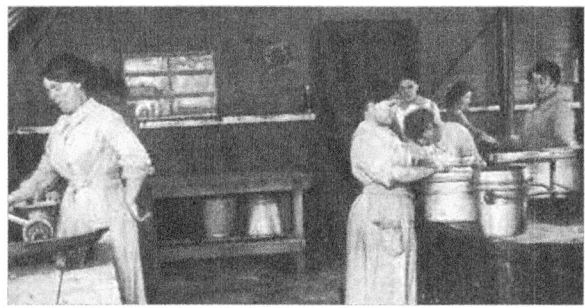

WAAC cooks at work at Camp No.1, Abbeville, 1917. (Private collection)

All these were the 'All quiet on the Western Front' circumstances. Very different conditions existed when the fighting was moving, or during the large Allied offensives. Before the major battles, the Somme in 1916, Ypres in 1917, soldiers would be well prepared in advance, and then issued with 'iron rations' for two days. What followed depended on the outcome of the battle. A further issue of 'iron rations', tepid or cold stew might be brought up in a hay box, or in a number of cases little or nothing more for a day or two, on occasions even three or four, until that phase of the battle was over or the unit itself was withdrawn from the fighting.

At base camps, some distance behind the front, ' women cooks', members of the newly formed Women's Army Auxiliary Corps, (W.A.A.C.) served as cooks, the first appearance of non-medical uniformed women units in a campaign theatre.

The worst period when soldiers suffered particularly severely from hunger was the Retreat from Mons in August-September 1914. Regiments were kept on the march in unusually hot weather with little or no rest from 24 August to 4 September. The British Expeditionary Force (B.E.F.) was placed on 'iron rations', bully beef, biscuits and tea packets for the Retreat. The briefest of halts, two or three hours, were permitted for sleep with much shorter periods for tea and biscuits. Occasionally, a few battalions were allowed to buy or acquire food, biscuits, tinned meat, jam and chocolate and a measure of wine from local villages on the road. The B.E.F. staff had deposited quarters of beef and biscuits by the sides of the roads but in the heat the meat had generally deteriorated, and the stocks were not always seen or were taken by local people, or later by advancing Germans. The Army that finally arrived on the Marne had marched on, dazed and fatigued, many staggering, some hallucinating and propped up by comrades, and all gnawed by hunger pains. Even during the First Battle of the Marne and First Ypres battle of September and October 1914 battalions were still living on 'iron rations' with perhaps a little jam for the biscuits but no hot food or even tea. However, with proper feeding restored, the 'Old Contemptibles' as the veterans of the Retreat were later to call themselves (a title arriving from the German Kaiser's remark that the British had only a contemptible little army), when restored to proper rations supplemented by visits to the local *estaminets* regiments returned very quickly to full fighting efficiency.

The great German offensives of 1918 forcing the British Fifth Army to withdraw in some confusion reduced regiments to basic 'iron rations', in some cases halved or absent for a day or two before the line was stabilised. Later, in some critical moments in July supplies, almost certainly including food, were dropped by the newly-formed Royal Air Force.

The last great Western Front battle, the Second Battle of the Marne, also saw some failure of rations to arrive for front line soldiers. The German attacks had by July 1918 created a huge salient reaching the Marne and in tremendous haste four British Army divisions were rushed to the support of the French, Italian and American forces containing the German attacks. The move was made in such haste that supply, and even the division's artillery, had to follow on a day or two later. The terrain, especially on the eastern side of the salient, was hilly and wooded, horse-drawn company cookers then had to be left behind and supplies when they arrived carried by mule. Some units here had for two or three days to fight on 'iron rations' or no rations at all, or whatever could be spared for them by the French. Of mules Kipling in his *Parade Song on the Screw-Gun Mules* wrote, 'For we can wriggle and climb, my lads, and turn up everywhere. And it's our delight on a mountain height with a leg or two to spare', a tribute to this overworked and long suffering animal well deserved here and in many other campaigns.

Over the four years of fighting the simple company field kitchens, the horses that drew them, and in France and elsewhere the humble mule, were almost as important a contribution to victory as the firearms.

3

The First World War: Other Theatres 1914–1918

Regiments of the British Army fought in six other theatres of operations beyond the Western Front. Two battalions participated in the four-year long campaign in German East Africa (now mainland Tanzania); larger formations fought on the Gallipoli peninsular and later in Macedonia; in Egypt, Palestine and Syria; and for a brief period in northern Italy. In the last months of the war and in 1918-19 the British Army was also involved in operations against the Bolsheviks in Russia.

Official accounts of food supplies are at best sketchy. Detail, however, can often be picked up from occasional sentences, sometimes just a few words, in accounts written by participants or from regimental histories.

East Africa 1914-18

The campaign in East Africa was mainly fought by black East and West African colonial regiments and Indian and South African troops. One Regular Army Lancashire battalion was involved from the outset, a very amateur Kitchener's Army battalion of Fusiliers arrived a little later. Neither had any experience of the enormous problems of tropical climate and terrain and suffered very severe casualty lists from disease. Food for them was based on the basic tin of meat, biscuits and a small piece of cheese; this was supplemented by local products, game birds and animals shot on the march, fruit including paw-paws, and maize meal bread or porridge; in some areas food was plentiful and well distributed, in many others there was poor distribution or nothing at all for several days. Thirst and water were generally a more serious problem than food to eat. Ox wagons had great difficulty in the terrain and to support the large force in the theatre supply was often human carriers, mostly recruited in the British East African Protectorate (Kenya). The needs of the African carriers were grossly neglected, at least 40,000 men dying of malnutrition and disease.

Gallipoli 1915-16

The brilliant idea behind the landings on the Gallipoli peninsula was to knock the Ottoman Empire, Turkey, out of the war by a quick stab at the heart of the empire, Constantinople, now Istanbul. Initially two landings on the west coast of the peninsula were made on 25 April 1915, one by British troops on several small beaches backed by low cliffs but with clear cliff paths, the second by the Australian and New Zealand Corps troops (ANZAC) in a badly selected area of a cove and small beaches with adjoining steep cliffs and hills. A third landing by British, Australian and New Zealand troops followed on 6 August in a bay surrounded by cliffs and hills, the Turks again holding the commanding heights. The campaign was under-resourced, badly prepared and badly led, with at times an almost unbelievable level of incompetency. It ended in failure, troops being withdrawn in January 1916.

The material conditions for the nine months of the campaign were often more testing than those on the Western Front, Turkish resistance was vigorous and fighting closer and more intense. The climate ranged from the chill winds and rain of spring to the sweltering heat of summer, and finally to the increasing cold, rain and winds of autumn and winter. The first landings, in particular those at Anzac Cove succeeded in gaining little more than beachheads, the hills and mountain spine of the peninsula providing the defender with decisive advantage and forcing the attackers into lives of closely packed and overcrowded trenches, dug-outs and caverns. The dead, soldiers and animals, could not always be removed from the battlefields, in heat decomposing. Myriads of flies and lice added seasonal tortures and lowered morale.

In these conditions water counted for more than food. There were few local wells, water as well as food had to be brought in by sea and for operational reasons could not always easily reach the front lines; it might have to be carried forward by soldiers the terrain being too difficult even for mules. In warm and hot weather a particularly serious problem arose when flies which had fed upon the putrefying corpses, men and animals, and on the trench latrines, alighted on food. Standing orders required all food, cooked or uncooked, to be protected, which was not always feasible in the operational conditions. A severe dysentery epidemic resulted, incapacitating hundreds of soldiers.

The First World War: Other Theatres 1914–1918

'The Anzac Walk' – Sick men queuing for rations, No 1 Field Ambulance, 'Brighton Beach', Gallipoli, 1915. (Australian War Memorial)

For the April landings troops were given a hot cooked meal on board the transport ships taking them to the peninsula. Survivors of the landings then found themselves in continuous fighting without respite for several days on end with their food at best bully beef, biscuits and 'black tea' (i.e. tea without milk), some units not even having these for one or two days. Field kitchens arrived later but operated under very great difficulty, Turkish artillery fire and the water shortage adding to the difficulties of out-loading and food preparation. For most of the campaign, although the supply was generally maintained, food was limited to bully beef, biscuits, the unpleasant plum and apple jam, tea and lime juice, with rum at irregular intervals. A greasy hot bully beef stew was far from suitable in the very hot summer weeks. Fruit and vegetables were almost non-existent locally and were not brought in by sea for many weeks. Diet became monotonous, depressing and soldiers showed signs of malnutrition and dehydration.

Regiments that landed in 6 August Suvla Bay assault were given a light 48 hours 'iron ration'. This scale may have been due to short supply or a belief that bully beef would simply melt in the tins, the weather being full August heat. This 'iron ration' consisted of a handful of small biscuits the size of an overcoat button, a small tin containing a cube of Oxo, half an ounce of tea and one ounce of sugar. After the fierce fighting of the landings conditions did improve. By mid-September tinned, meat usually Maconochie's stew, biscuits, occasionally rice and jam, bacon, dried potatoes and onions were being provided and small quantities of locally grown figs and melons were 'acquired'. Tea, now sometimes with condensed milk, was in generous supply, cigarettes, however, were scarce. The diet became very monotonous, in conditions which provided no relief via a local *estaminet*. The change from the heat of summer to the early cold of winter led to an outbreak of jaundice for which the limited ration issues were also in part responsible.

The withdrawal and re-embarkation into ships was carried out with a professional skill that stood in marked contrast to command during the campaign itself. At Suvla ration boxes fitted only with sand were landed to deceive the Turks.

Mesopotamia 1915-17

The extraordinarily difficult conditions for soldiers fighting a campaign in Iraq, in the First World War called Mesopotamia, will be familiar to late twentieth and early twenty-first century generations of British soldiers. The temperatures could vary from a sapping 125 degree Fahrenheit in the shade in the June to September summer, down to 18 degrees in January to February, when there was only limited food that could be obtained locally. The British soldier of 1991 was able to prepare for and fight in battle reasonably well prepared, his predecessor in 1915 was wretchedly prepared.

In the First World War there were two sets of operations in Mesopotamia against the Turks, opening with the first battles in the south and the advance, siege and surrender of the town of Kut El Amara, the second a somewhat better prepared campaign moving up the Tigris River to Baghdad and beyond. In the first set of operation opening on 19 November there were two, later three divisions based around Indian Army regiments but including some eight battalions of British infantry, with artillery batteries, engineers and service units all poorly equipped. The early fighting against the even worse equipped Turks was successful but the march on Kut urged on by ambitious and foolhardy generals, most notably General Townshend, was to prove a disaster. Even before the division had been besieged in Kut, the privations of the ordinary soldiers in conditions of the heat and thirst, dirt and mosquitoes and flies, were appalling, sunstroke, malaria and dysentery incapacitating many. Supply transport was by water, boats and then on by mules but in March to May flood created large areas of swamps. Food was served out on halts on the march.

The nine week long approach march to Kut of one division including three British battalions involved hard fighting but was also an indication of the food problems to come. For most of the march soldiers were limited to bully beef and biscuits or bread and tea. In the early days when the weather was still very hot, bully beef melted in the tins, fresh meat when obtained locally often included maggots.

On occasions sand grouse were shot to provide good fresh meat. Cooking stews was done over fires, Camelthorn being used as a fuel. No local fruit or vegetables were available at the time. The British soldiers began to suffer from beri beri, a vitamin B1 deficiency malnutrition disease; this at first causes breathlessness, eyesight problems, rapid heartbeat and nervous conditions which could lead on to swollen legs and arms, swollen livers and in a number of cases death.

The division entered Kut, a town on a bend of the river, in the first days of December 1915. Almost immediately the Turks besieged the garrison, a force of growing strength holding the land approach and using vessels, guns and obstacles to block the river approach. The garrison began a life under regular artillery bombardments and machine gun fire, soon supplemented by aircraft bombing, days in dug-outs, individuals picked off by snipers, bitterly cold weather, flood water when the rainy season began, the floods together with lice at the outset followed by fleas, mosquitoes and sand flies from mid-January.

The siege to last 147 days was perhaps the worst combat experience suffered by British and Indian troops in the twentieth century. Townshend unwisely allowed a full ration scale for the first weeks. Troops briefly lived well: one pound of meat, one pound of bread, three ounces of bacon, four ounces of onions, six ounces of potatoes, three ounces of jam, butter, salt, cheese and a quart of water per day. Units in the perimeter front line were supplied by men from the second line by handcart. The wooden doors and rafters of the houses of Arab inhabitants were pulled down for firewood.

By January, however, the first relief attempts had failed. Supply had been cut by floods and mud with the soldiers of one regiment reduced to a couple of biscuits and tea for two days in heavy rain. Everywhere the weather became colder and wetter. In Kut half rations were ordered and in February Arab town dwellers houses were searched for stocks of grain, a half of stock being requisitioned. In late January began the melancholy business of a certain number of the few oxen and more numerous horses and mules being killed and made into stews thickened by potato meal as long as potatoes lasted. Meat from a well-fed mule was seen as acceptable, from less well fed animals, mules and oxen it was often very stringy. Starlings were shot and cooked. Vegetables were no longer available. Tobacco was made from any local green leaves, dried and mixed with sawdust and ginger. Sugar ran out. Mills of large stones, powered by donkeys or an engine improvised by a small team from the Royal Flying Corps (R.F.C.), ground barley and wheat for bread. Water was baled out of the Tigris, sometimes under fire. A barge on the Tigris full of crude oil was seized, the oil used for cooking. A shortage of salt by the end of February made the horse-meat much less palatable. The first to suffer from scurvy were the

Indian soldiers who for a long time refused to eat meat for religious reasons. British soldiers soon followed.

In the last two months conditions steadily worsened. The bread ration was reduced from eight to five and then to four ounces per day, meat to one pound of horse flesh, jam to an ounce with perhaps a small issue of dates and tea. Local grasses were cut to make a form of spinach, not all the grasses were edible and soldiers who ate the wrong grass developed enteritis. The R.F.C. briefly attempted an air drop of food, the first in military history, but the quantities were totally inadequate, some falling into the Tigris or to the Turks. By mid-March tea had run out to be replaced by boiled ginger. In desperation soldiers were reduced to horse livers and hearts, the boiling of animal heads, scavenging for bones to pick, frying dogs and cats, even hedgehogs, in axle grease and tobacco now being only from grasses or apricot tree leaves. Disease and physical weakness lowered any remaining energy soldiers had left to fight, men fainting, collapsing with dysentery and scurvy spreading. Legs and arms became thinner and thinner, faces sunken and hollow-eyed. In the last week the garrison was reduced to a few small biscuits per day. Surrender was inevitable and followed on 26 April 1916, with many hundreds of men dying in brutal captivity over the next two years.

The second campaign, opening in December 1916 with the troops entering Baghdad on 17 March 1917, was much better organised, with a more powerful force, some 300,000 men, able commanders, and improved supply; lessons had been learnt. A ship for carrying refrigerated meat was sent out from Britain. A daily ration more like that of Western Front soldiers and including tin fruit and condensed milk was laid down and to combat scurvy. Lentils, peas and Marmite were included. The Royal Army Service Corps official history records machines imported for the manufacture of soda water and ice and the importing of labour for dairy and chicken farms and vegetable gardens. Food was carried forward to advancing formations and units by petrol driven lorries and by boat to temporary riverhead supply dumps. Front line soldiers emergency 'iron rations' were soon supplemented regularly with chicken, butter, milk, apples, apples and apricots and tomatoes, cucumber, onions and soda water. Casualties from disease were in consequence very much lower.

Egypt, Palestine, Syria 1915-19

It was not until 1917 that British and imperial forces defending the Suez Canal were able to advance from Egypt into Palestine and on to Syria. General Allenby's regiments were better provided with tea, meat, bacon, grain, beans, dried fruit and potatoes from Cyprus and Sudan to supplement bully beef, biscuits, jam and tea. Water was a much more serious problem than food, thirst the common and sometimes extreme condition. On reaching the Jaffa area local unleavened bread, oranges, figs and other fruit was available for purchase or on occasional pillage. From the outset the Army in Egypt had been provided with insulated boxes to keep meat fresh but the bully beef was often liquefied in the heat. There were nevertheless periods either for operational or transport reasons when troops were placed on half rations, or a diet of biscuits, cheese, dates and cocoa, but there was never the prolonged hardship of the Mesopotamia campaign. Stews, where possible flavoured with a local spice, were popular. When not in the front line army canteens provided sardines, milk, chocolate and fruit. Transport of food to forward units was generally by motor lorry or horse drawn wagons, on one occasion by air drop. In the muddy autumn season that notoriously difficult animal, the camel had to be used, but even these could slip, upsetting their loads in the mud. Again the words of Kipling's, *The Commissariat Camel's* song: "Somebody's load has slipped off in the road, cheer for a halt and a row! Urr! Yarrh! Grr! Arrh! Somebody's catching it now" paint the transport picture. An unusual feature of the campaign was the use for deception not only of dummy horses and men, but also fake bivouac fires and dust clouds created by mules to simulate mounted troops going for water.

Camel supply, Palestine Campaign, 1918. (Crown Copyright)

Macedonia 1915-18

A British contingent, at its peak eight divisions, was sent to join the larger French led force landing at Salonika in Greece with the objectives on the east entering Bulgaria and the Turkish Ottoman Empire, and on the west with fortune advancing into Macedonia, Kosovo and Serbia, the operation lasted from 1915 to 1918.

The terrain was of increasing difficulty the further the force moved inland, relatively flat if swampy areas gave way to hills, rocks and mountains, the ground being a wilderness of thickets, brambles, with only a few woods. The best roads were little more than tracks, the worst causing constant upsets of supply carts pulled by mules. Water was in short supply, more mules were required to pull water tanks, and soldiers in hot weather commented that such heavy chlorinated water as they received was warm, parching throats and mouths. The climate ranged from extreme cold in winter to sweltering heat in the summer. The worst local hazard facing the force was, however, gnats, mosquitoes and malaria, the latter creating sudden deaths, huge casualty lists and for many (including this author's father) recurrent bouts for the remainder of their lives. Food supplies were often delayed by shipping problems at sea and on the ground the shortage of wood for cooking fires, in the event fuel often reduced to bundles of dried sticks and brambles collected and carried by soldiers on the march, or the use of packing cases. The 'Aldershot Oven' was found to be unsuitable and an improved 'Perkins cooker' was introduced.

A field bakery using the Aldershot Oven, Salonika, 1915. (Crown Copyright)

Local produce varied, Macedonia was a very poor territory. Most villagers were too poor to help, but on occasions and in season mutton, tomatoes, eggs, pomegranates, figs, apricots and melons with also beer and spirits could be purchases. Hares and partridges were shot on the march, the occasional Bulgar sheep also provided good fresh meat. In season blackberries were picked to make jam. In the early stages of the campaign before supplies were properly organised soldiers had to fight for two or more days without rations. Later for much of the campaign and in particular in the winters, front line soldiers were back to the basics of lumps of bully beef floating in greasy water, biscuits, tea plus with fortune a little jam and also with fortune a small but strong 10 percent oven proof Jamaican rum ration. Sometimes boiled rice was available for a second light meal. Operations permitting, food supplies were sent to 'dumps' by lorry, mule wagon or mule packs; these might contain tinned fish, condensed milk, bread, meat, onions and potatoes for stews, peaches, more jam, sugar and tea. Predictably some claimed that much of the best had been appropriated by the supply troops; such suspicion will exist until armies exist no more. Experienced units, though, did avoid sending newly arrived soldiers to the 'dump' to collect their unit's allocation. If for example the meat supply was part fresh and part bully, the experienced soldier would ensure that his unit got the best. These 'dumps' were protected from German air attack by balloons filled with explosives.

As the campaign progressed Expeditionary Force Canteens, some large and some small, were opened on the main tracks for use by soldiers in rest periods or quiet times. Officers', sergeants' and corporals' and soldiers' messes would club together to buy what was on offer. One at a small town, Janes, supplying troops on the Lake Doiran front not too far from Salonika, was able to sell over 300 items. These were mainly practical such as handkerchiefs, towels and soap, but the foods for sale could include sausages, tinned haddock, lard, lentils and honey and tobacco.

Such facilities were of course only available in quiet periods and the weather permitting. Closer to reality was the observation of one soldier who had carried 'iron rations' over many miles: "All the time you have it you know that you are assured against starvation so you must keep it and never eat it, under pain of dreadful penalties for it is only designed to last for one day, and [once] that is over you are finished forever."

Italy 1917-18

The Italian Army fighting the Austrians in the mountains of northern Italy suffered a disastrous defeat in October 1917. British and French divisions had to be sent to support the demoralised and ineptly led Italians. The four British divisions arriving in November were well supplied by lorries driven by Italian drivers accustomed to winding mountain roads. Some groceries came from France, flour and preserved foreign meat from Britain, fruit and vegetables were purchased locally, and two field butchers and two field bakeries supplied many detachments for forward formations and units. Canteens were opened for units in rest periods. Soldiers welcomed the change from the Western Front.

Cigarettes appear to have been in limited supply but for food it was claimed than on only two days were British troops reduced to emergency 'iron rations'.

North Russia 1918-19

British and contingents from a number Allied forces were sent to North Russia from June 1918 in the hope that by supporting local anti-British Bolshevik forces they would prevent the triumph of Bolsheviks and also to ensure the two north Russian ports, Murmansk and Archangel, were not used by German submarines.

The conditions were difficult with a short late May to September summer, and mud floods followed in late September, ice was on the rivers in October, with frozen rivers and bitter cold to April and May. In the summer there was hardly any darkness, in winter hardly any daylight. Seasonal summer insects included mosquitoes and gnats in clouds. Transport for food supplies included, in season, river barges, ponies pulling *droskies* (open four-wheeled horse-drawn carriages) and motor vehicles. In cold weather the Army had recourse to reindeers; these, however, like the South African oxen, had a very rigid biological clock—requiring at least half a day in a forest area for their food, tree lichen, together with a fresh forest everyday. Teams of four, three in front and one behind as a brake with a Laplander driver, could pull a sleigh carrying a 600lb load over snow on hills and rough ground to deliver food and supplies to outlying detachments. Occasionally unlucky reindeer were required to provide meat to supplement rations.

All these conditions led regiments who thought after the November 1918 Armistice that the war was over back to trenches, bully beef, Maconochie, margarine or lard, biscuits made into porridge with jam, dates, and tea together with a rum issue for much of the time. Very occasionally salmon and other fresh fish became available. No local fruit or vegetables were available though some were imported from Britain together with peas, oatmeal, cheese and soup. Three ounces of lime juice were provided four days each week. The Army also opened a small farm in June 1919 growing potatoes, peas, mustard and cress, lettuce and cabbage, but the quantities produced were limited and insufficient for the forces. Troops suffered from malnutrition, and complained about the monotony of the food. As chances of the force serving any useful purpose faded away regiments were withdrawn in September and October 1919.

An interesting feature of the operations, foreshadowing future developments, was the use of expert advice from the Antarctic explorer, Sir Ernest Shackleton, on the foods to be included in rations for cold weather warfare.

4

The Inter-War Years: 1919–1939

In the years between the major world wars the established strength of the Regular Army was progressively reduced to a little over 200,000, but many regiments remained under strength. The Army was engaged in a wide variety of internal security, 'imperial policing' duties in Britain's huge overseas empire. In most of these a normal food supply was provided for soldiers either in barracks or by mobile field kitchens of the 1914-18 war pattern supplemented by local purchases. Two campaigns, however, were particularly difficult; first, the suppression of a major revolt in Iraq in 1920, where regiments encountered the same problems as the columns advancing to the relief of Kut and onwards to Baghdad had faced in the war. The second was the suppression of an uprising in 1931 in Burma where battalions, British and Indian, fighting in the jungle had to be supplied by elephant; one animal could carry three days' worth of food, water and supplies for a platoon on jungle patrolling.

In Britain until the late 1930s, the soldier lived in nineteenth, sometimes eighteenth, century barracks or 1915 Army corrugated iron blocks refurbished with a coat of dark green paint, his food prepared on coal fired ranges. In 1921 an official peacetime barracks ration scale was authorised, providing per day:

12 ozs of meat
16 ozs of bread
2 ozs of bacon

Plus a small cash allowance for quartermasters to buy any supplement which tended to be spent on sugar rather than meat. In practice, for the ordinary infantry private, trooper or gunner this might mean a breakfast at 06.30 or 07.00 of two boiled eggs or two rashers of bacon, mushy tomatoes, some bread with poor quality margarine and tea. Out on training there followed a haversack lunch of two sandwiches of very thickly cut bread and margarine filled with corned beef or cheese and a slab of fruit cake or an apple. Training ended with tea and bread at 16.00 or shortly afterwards. Inevitably soldiers had to spend part of their pay on a more substantial evening meal in a National Army and Air Force Institutes (NAAFI) canteen where food stuffs were available at wholesale prices. On occasions a 1914-18 field kitchen would provide food, usually stews, bread and tea; on some exercises a NAAFI field canteen would follow. All this may appear very poor for the present day reader but in the context of the period it was food for real, for many unemployed there was none elsewhere. Hundreds joined the Army to escape hunger, regimental depots having to run programmes to build up men's physical strength before proper military training could begin.

Territorial Army training on a No 1 Cooker, 1939. (Royal Logistics Corps)

Reform came in 1937, following the arrival of Leslie Hore-Belisha at the War Office as Secretary of State, the first to give a very high priority to the welfare of the rank and file. He appointed Sir Isidore Salmon, the Chairman of the famous Lyons Teas Shops organisation, to be his Honorary Advisor on Catering and a wide range of reform, not always well received by more traditionally minded service officers, followed. A proper supper meal was introduced in March 1938. Later in 1938 the Catering Manager of Trust House Hotels, Richard Byford, was appointed Chief Inspector of Army Catering, a new post at Salmon's request. Byford set to work immediately to develop the Aldershot Army School of Catering, replacing many old barrack kitchens and installing gas cookers instead of coal ranges. Cooks were at last recognised as military tradesmen and given craft pay, and in 1939 managers recruited from industry became catering training officers.

Other developments to be of great value were the ending of horse transport—the B.E.F. that went to France in September 1939 was, for all its faults, entirely moved on petrol-equipped vehicles—and the issue of mobile petrol cookers transportable on the backs of three ton lorries. Three types of these mobile cookers were developed. Cooker Portable No 1 could cook for any number up to 125, No 2 was intended for small 8-10 men detachments, and No 3 for 15. All were great improvements on the old company cooker but each had small technical faults, No 2 and No 3 were not sufficiently robust, and the numbers available at the outbreak of the Second World War were inadequate. Guidance was also issued on the preparation of stews, pies and puddings in camp kettles.

Although not directly related to the Army, inter-war years' research by a number of leading experts who had been engaged in research on the food available to the nation's poor, notably, Sir John Boyd Orr and Jack Drummond, highlighted serious nutritional deficiencies. The experiences of Arctic and Antarctic explorers, notably Quintin Riley, of packed composite rations were also to prove of the greatest importance almost immediately in the war years.

5

The Second World War: 1939–1942

The 'Phoney War', Norway 1940

For once the outbreak of war on 3 September 1939 saw a novel problem, that of feeding troops in the field on active service within the United Kingdom itself. Two anti-aircraft artillery divisions broken down into numerous batteries of A.A. gun, searchlight and listening device detachments scattered around fields near London and a few other cities were mainly manned by men, and later women, from Territorial Army units that had no provision for unit cooking, staff and limited experience of living in the field in worsening weather. Food of course was to hand, but serving it hot was essential for efficiency and morale. Some units were able to build the 1900s type Aldershot field kitchens, others had for some time to improvise with braziers made from oil drums and buckets, waste oil from vehicle sumps being used as fuel if no coal or charcoal was available, again others more fortunate were able to use the new Portable Cookers with camp kettles, or hay boxes for outlying detachments. A manual set out simple recipes for stews with vegetables and for puddings. After the fall of France and the opening of German air attacks on several key cities more men and women were deployed in anti-aircraft defences, and now also in coast defence artillery batteries. The men in these latter units could often be fed from nearby houses requisitioned for billeting, or in some cases in nineteenth century fortifications built to secure the realm against earlier invasion threats. The basic First World War rations, the 1917 higher scale and the 24 hour emergency ration pack remained unaltered throughout the remaining months of 1939.

Regiments sent to Norway in April and May 1940 following the German invasion on 9 April 1940 arrived ill-prepared for late winter and early spring conditions, very sharp penetrating cold, winds and in the north snow. Regiments landed with little more than bully beef and biscuits or an early form of compo ration packs, tinned meat and vegetables and small quantities of biscuits, cheese, sugar

Soldiers of the British Expeditionary Force in France drawing food from a protected field kitchen, 1939. (Royal Logistics Corps)

and tea, together with any chocolate that wise soldiers would have bought before leaving England. No field cooking equipment arrived with most of the landings. Regiments found on arrival that the Norwegians at the harbours were happy to give or sell dried fish, vegetables, eggs, potatoes and rye bread. An Aldershot oven field bakery to supply the force tasked to take Narvik was set up —after several feet of snow had first been cleared. The advances made following the two southern landings were very soon to be followed by a hurried and confused withdrawal, and infantry troops were faced with attacks from the air and by advancing German armour. Feeding became occasional; on some days units could cook one hot meal a day, more often this was not feasible and some special force companies had to survive on Marmite and cocoa. When possible soldiers scrounged food, ham, cheese or just rye bread from deserted farms and village inns but some rural areas were very poor. Most, but not those soldiers killed or captured, passed, to use one survivor's phrase, through "a barrier of pain and hunger" before reaching their evacuation ships.

Defence of the United Kingdom and Home Service

In the first four months of 1940 strong pressure headed by the Treasury led to scale reductions in basic commodities for soldiers stationed in the United Kingdom in particular, to ten ounces of meat, one and a half-ounces of bacon and twelve ounces of bread per day (there was even a suggestion that cocoa replace meat and dates replace sugar). It was also decided that provision for women soldiers should be four-fifths of that for a man. Later in the summer an improved Home Service Office Ration Scale was introduced based on a provision of 4,000 calories per day but retaining the four-fifths level for women at a slightly lower calorie level. Evidently women personnel found this unsatisfactory as it was soon changed to a separate and improved scale for women with slightly less meat but more fruit and vegetables. The Home Service Scales provided for a cooked breakfast, a midday and an evening meal, with units generally subscribing funds to keep local NAAFI prices low for extra food and beer.

As the war progressed and severe rationing was imposed on the civil population more reductions followed, bread to ten ounces and meat to eight, with in 1941 a new fixed scale which with a few further small reductions remained for the rest of the war. This March 1941 daily scale was that provided for soldiers training, awaiting embarkation or in anti-aircraft or coast defence.

Meat	6oz	men	5 ¾ oz	women
Bacon	12/7 oz	men	1 1/7 oz	women
Offal or sausages	15/7 oz	men	11/7 oz	women (sausages only)
Bread	10 oz	men	7 oz	women
Flour	2 oz	men	2 oz	women
Butter or margarine	1½ oz	men	1½ oz	women
Cheese	4/7 oz	men	4/7 oz	women
Milk	3 oz	men	3¼ oz	women
Sugar	2 oz	men	2 oz	women
Potatoes	13 oz	men	12 oz	women
Fresh vegetables	55/7 oz	men	8 oz	women
Tea	2/7 oz	men	2/7 oz	women

The margarine was now strengthened with concentrates of Vitamins A and D. A practical difficulty, however, remained. In some circumstances items on the scale could only be obtained in commercially produced tins. These were not always suitable, either in the box packaging in which they were delivered or the tins themselves for flexible handling and distribution in operational conditions. Biscuits in particular could vary greatly in quality, the well-known British brands generally excellent but some imported brands being very poor.

Throughout the war the Army paid increasing attention to the training of cooks, both regimental and when formed in 1941, of the Army Catering Corps with its own cap badge and identity. Courses were held regularly in all theatres and several overseas schools of cookery opened. Ration scales for different theatres and climates some rather belatedly, and separate scales for women, were set out. Training included exercises of cooking under operational conditions, and trade testing in the United Kingdom, the Middle East and India. Special study and improvements went to the needs of small, platoon or smaller, size of detachments of men and to meet the needs of more mobile warfare.

France May-June 1940

The nine British Expeditionary Force (B.E.F.) divisions that advanced into Belgium in May 1940 had enjoyed a regular pre-war scale supply of good issue food well supplemented by local purchases and soldier's own personal local shopping until the German offensive broke upon them on 10 May. At first the advancing regiments continued to eat quality food prepared at unit level until they became locked into combat, amidst chaotic conditions of ferocious attacks from German troops, armour and aircraft and the roads crowded with the ever increasing number of the Belgian and French civilian refugee 'Exodus'. Regiments were then reduced to emergency ration tinned meat and vegetables and biscuits—if these could actually be delivered. At the start of the retreat catering centres were set up at railway stations and on the roads to the coast, together with hurriedly formed transit camps. These however could not last long in the face of the speed of the German advance, forcing frontline regiments into retreat, often rapid and sometimes disorganised. The Commander-in-Chief, Lord Gort, ordered half rations on 26 May but by that time many soldiers had been without a hot meal, or even a meal at all, for two days on the march and were taking anything they could acquire from farms and small towns and villages on their way to the coast. Some regiments had lucky finds in a well-stocked shop or farm or abandoned bakeries or butcheries, together with the few hours respite necessary to prepare a roast chicken or pig meal, others were soon reduced to biscuits. Matters were not helped by demoralised French soldiers looting any British ration dump they came across in their withdrawal or flight. In the strain and chaos of the weight of the German attacks battalions became increasingly split up, losing contact with their neighbouring units and often some of their own companies.

The army that arrived in the Dunkirk perimeter was, then, badly exhausted, bewildered, demoralised, dehydrated and very hungry. It arrived disorganised, in units, in sub-units, and detachments that had become separated—and soldiers that had detached themselves defensively proclaiming that they were the sole survivors of their unit. In some units officers had wisely ordered men to collect or acquire any food they could in the final stages of their retreat, anticipating that there would be little available on the beaches. Fortunately the administrative staff had the foresight to arrange for 80,000 gallons of water to be stockpiled in cans placed at intervals among the Dunkirk sand dunes. Royal Navy ships deposited consignments of ration packs on some beaches and in the docks. A few civilian aircraft were requisitioned to drop food, but the quantities were small. These naval and air supplies were distributed to separate Army Corps rendezvous and cookhouses were set up for a few hundred fortunate men. Abandoned canteen vehicles yielded bully beef, biscuits and condensed milk for some lucky finders, even ordinary abandoned military vehicles contained cigarettes that departing drivers in a hurry had left behind.

The Dunkirk beaches during the evacuation, from 19 May to 5 June, though, were for the large majority of ordinary soldiers a story of patient disciplined waiting while under German air attack, and of hunger in varying degrees. Crews of ships, large and small, were able to arrive with humble contributions of biscuits, the occasional tin of meat or a sandwich for their passengers. Little else was available. Morale was not helped by the fact that the B.E.F.'s rear units and logistic staffs were the first to be evacuated, battered regiments of desperately hungry and weary men were not impressed when told by the remarkably efficient beach organisation that they must wait their turn. The more fortunate had their first taste of good food again aboard Royal Navy warships, the less fortunate aboard the *ad hoc* collection of ships assembled for the evacuation had only the consolation of being alive until they reached the well organised reception arrangements in Britain.

Malta 1940-42

The besieging of Malta began with the Italian entry into the war on 10 June 1940. For the first few months the island's population and the Army's garrison, of a number of infantry and artillery units, suffered little more than inconvenience in respect of food, enjoying supplies built up before June 1940. Shortages began to become serious in 1941, compounded of course by continual air attacks. Petrol and vehicle spare parts ran short, mules being used increasingly to transport food and water. Regiments reared rabbits and chickens, and grew vegetables. In 1942 conditions greatly worsened, especially following the advance of the Afrika Korps towards Egypt and the failure of the island's potato crop, which had been abundant in 1941. Bread had to be made from yeast brought in by submarine or dropped from the air, and then mixed with potato balm. Lord Gort, arriving as Governor in May, ordered troops onto half rations, described in practice as 'a tiny piece of bully beef, some dehydrated potatoes and a small piece of bread' per day. The breweries were out of action early, available though was an unpalatable local wine, *Amreet*, called '*Stuka Juice*' by the garrison. Very occasionally an aircraft could bring in limited supplies of cigarettes and chocolate. The food shortage preyed on everyone's minds, and in a few cases Court Martials followed cases of robbery. After the August 1942 'Pedestal' naval convoy and the Allied landings in North Africa conditions slowly began to ease, and from 7 December rations were increased to provide one ounce of oatmeal flour four times a week, one ounce of bread and three to five ounces of butter per day. By 1943 the battalions had been withdrawn and more normal feeding restored for remaining troops.

The malnutrition during the siege caused outbreaks of sandfly fever and dysentery in the battalions. One battalion, of the Devonshire Regiment, estimated that across the unit the average individual loss of weight had been two stones.

Siege of Malta. A Maltese adaptation of the Aldershot Oven for a bakery used in the siege, 1940-43. (Royal Logistics Corps)

The Middle East 1940-42

The popular image of the 'Desert War' campaigns in Egypt and Libya is one of clean warfare in open desert, few civilians and the rival armies fighting professionally and honourably. While this image is very largely true it was nevertheless tough campaigning for the rank and file. Often in scorching heat, but with rainstorms and in the winter nights of bitter cold, soldiers might be fighting in sweat-soaked shirts and shorts or shivering in the inadequate light khaki drill uniform supplemented only by a pullover. Flies, fleas, dust and sandstorms were part of daily life. The Middle East Field Service ration scale was designed to provide an average basic 3,700 calories per day but only 3,100 for those in action. The reality proved to be rather different.

A British tank crew having a 'brew up' in North Africa, c 1941. (National Archives)

Most serious of all from the soldier's point of view was the permanent shortage of water, thirst being almost always present and the demand and need for a brew-up of tea always pressing. Little local supply was available, much had to be brought forward by water tank lorry or landed from ships. Even if these were not attacked by the enemy problems abounded, especially in the case of lorries, these frequently losing their way and arriving late, on several occasions not at all, forever lost in the desert. A water pipeline 145 miles long was completed in December 1941, but was, of course, lost six months later. The water was at best chlorinated, or the product of a desalination process that left an unpleasant taste and caused any milk available to curdle in lumps at the bottom of a cup or mug of tea, a taste that had to be acquired. From the lorries water had to be taken forward to units and detachments in cans, tins or captured jerry cans. For much of the Western Desert Campaign the soldier was reduced to six, sometimes four, pints of water a day for all purposes, drinking, washing, cleaning shirts and shorts. To maintain food supplies for the field service ration scale and base troops local resources were developed in Egypt for potato growing, fish curing, pig farming, dehydration and canning of vegetables and the importing of cattle from Sudan. Processing, tinning and refrigeration storage facilities were in time developed.

The response to the Italian attempt to invade Egypt in September 1940 began a learning curve for the British Army; it also provided the first examples of an occasional benefit to a lucky few soldiers' diet, captured Italian food, especially in the well-stocked stores of senior Italian officers, good tinned meats, soups, cheeses, sauces, wines and spirits. But for the rank and file majority of soldiers the two years of fighting were years of bully beef or tinned meat and vegetable stew, tea, condensed milk, biscuits and lime juice or Vitamin C tablets, with very infrequent variation. In rear areas small scale bartering or buying could secure an egg, often rather stale, for a soldier; also in rear and rest areas Expeditionary Force Institute canteens manned by civilians offered more homely fare. On the two brief occasions when Benghazi was in British hands fresh fruit and potatoes were landed by sea, vegetables, however, deteriorated too quickly.

Egypt and Libya saw three campaigns. The first under General Sir Archibald Wavell, saw the repulse of the early Italian attack and in September the opening of a victorious offensive by the 'Army of the Nile' clearing the Italians out of Benghazi and all Cyrenaica (Eastern Libya). This promising offensive had to halt as formations were removed from the Army to support Greece, threatened and then attacked by the Germans. As the troops departed for Greece General Erwin Rommel arrived with the Afrika Korps and pushed Wavell's Army back to its start line on the Egypt Libya border but leaving a besieged garrison at Tobruk. There followed in November 1941 General Sir Claude Auchinleck's offensive relieving Tobruk and once again occupying eastern Libya in a short-lived triumph, turning quickly to defeat with in July 1942 the Army forced back deep into Egypt threatening Alexandria. The hurried early 1942 retreat from Libya, involving six weeks of fighting in which few supplies could be sent forward produced specific symptoms of malnutrition. Soldiers were urged to take Vitamin B and C pills. The tide was finally turned by General Sir Bernard Montgomery's morale restored and rebranded Eighth Army victory at El Alamein in October 1942 leading to the ejection of all German and Italian forces from Libya by December.

Even when the fighting was not fast moving the local conditions made preparation of the one daily cooked meal difficult. The three portable cookers proved unsatisfactory, sand and grit often clogging the oven burners out in the open. An improvised field kitchen was devised based on an adapted three-ton lorry fitted with metal sides to counter sand blown by the winds, and fitted with five clamped hay boxes, a No 1 cooker and six gallon food containers, capable of providing a hot meal for 130. In the event of strong winds and sand storms other lorries would be parked in a protective shield around the lorry with the cookers. Operational conditions, fumes, ventilation and light that could give away a position usually meant that only one hot meal, breakfast or dinner, could be provided and problems still remained for small outlying reconnaissance detachments where men were often exhausted after battle and the fumes within their tanks, the crews preferring rest rather than food and not welcoming the requirement to cook their own food. At nightfall armoured regiments would form a laager, headquarters in the centre and tank squadrons around it, guns facing outward. A common pattern of feeding for these regiments provided for one of the regiment's majors to bring the food forward from rear supply columns or parks, and then a subaltern to distribute it to the squadrons. In some units tea could be prepared at reveille with a slice of cold meat and biscuits later in the morning, the day ending with a cooked meal at 7.30 p.m. If the regiment was very close to the enemy cooking of food or even a hot cup of tea became impossible. Hay boxes were tried, but were not a success for those armoured regiments that had advanced forward over considerable distances, the long journey for food prepared many hours previously arriving cold and unpalatable, even if it could be delivered at all. Water supply generally only permitted three cups of tea per day but a rum issue was sometimes to hand. A highly successful improvisation that came to be used widely in quiet periods of the war was the 'Benghazi Burner'; sand was placed in the bottom of former jam or biscuit tins or a petrol can large enough to support a kettle and petrol poured over the sand and set alight. Using a sufficiently large tin three gallons of hot water or three gallons of the meat and vegetable stew could be prepared though one may wonder whether some flavour of petrol may have also been present. Another remarkable improvisation was the tying of a can of water to the tank's exhaust so that when the tank could stop tea leaves could be put in immediately, and the crew have a quick mug of tea at any pause in a battle. In late 1942 an improved petrol cooker, the 'Hydra', that could be used in the backs of ordinary three ton lorries, became available. The Germans evidently had very similar problems and it seems that if in the desert a German and a British supply column met there would be no action by tacit mutual consent. This of course did not apply to supply columns met by their enemy's front line units.

The seven month long 1941 siege of Tobruk was a far more fortunate affair than Ladysmith or Kut El Amara. The town, being on the coast with small port facilities, the Royal Navy, albeit at some considerable cost in ships, was able to keep the garrison supplied.

Loading valuable food supplies onto trucks during the retreat from Libya.
(Royal Logistics Corps)

Life for the garrison was one of living in dug-outs, cavities, holes in the ground and shelters made from the ruin of Tobruk's buildings. German artillery and aircraft bombarded regularly adding to the all-pervading dust, near the perimeter's edge snipers were active. There were, in some sectors of the perimeter, tacit, unwritten and not signalled two-hour ceasefires in the evenings when some on each side could emerge from dug-outs, stretch legs and perhaps cook a meal of biscuit porridge made from crushed biscuits—though many still had to cook in dug-outs. For the garrison water remained a problem, though the town of Tobruk had a local desalination plant which was put to use, in practice though the majority of soldiers on most days received approximately six pints. The Navy's food supplies were unloaded at night and sent to a depot near the harbour from which units drew supplies to distribute to dug-outs and platoons from which sections would appear for their hot meal turn by turn, generally in daylight hours. The actual food remained based on a bully beef, biscuits and small quantities of margarine (unfortunately deficient in Vitamin A), tea, sugar and jam together with initially ascorbic acid Vitamin C tablets and later lime juice. Occasionally this was supplemented by fresh meat, live sheep having been landed from ships, dug-out baked bread often with weevils referred to as 'meat loaf', and fruit and vegetables, usually tinned but occasionally fresh. Men going out on patrol would be given a priority hot meal and a tot of rum. The garrison's Australian units offered culinary expertise in developing variants on the basic commodities, a particularly popular dish being 'dog fritters', in which biscuits swollen to four times their issue size following a soaking in water were sliced down the middle, filled with jam and fried. Small 'one off' one-day issues of flour, bacon, rice or potatoes gave cooks the occasional opportunity to vary the monotony of bully beef and biscuits. The garrison did not experience malnutrition and when the town was reoccupied later the land surrounding dug-outs was found to contain unused food hidden away by the former defenders.

Rommel's very successful offensive in the summer of 1942 bringing the Afrika Korps close to Alexandria forced the Army back on emergency bully beef, biscuits and tea with little else, particularly after the loss of the big store depot at Mersa Matruh, all contributing to very low morale. By the autumn, however, supply of both water and food, now including more and better margarine and bacon, and morale had been restored and the Army that attacked at Alamein was a reinvigorated force.

The Middle East Command had other campaigns to wage in its theatres of which the two most important were that against the Italian East African empire from 1940-42, and against the Vichy French regime in Syria and Lebanon in June and July 1941. From the point of view of food supply to front-line soldiers, both campaigns were bully beef, biscuits, tea and lime juice-based, though in the final stages of both local fresh fruit became available and a local bakery established. Transport from railheads was where possible by lorry, otherwise by mule or camel. Mules were also used to carry supplies that had been loaded on commandeered dhows in Port Sudan and unloaded in small bays on the Eritrean coast. The long supply journeys though led to any fruit or vegetables arriving rotten.

The most severe fighting was against the very resolute and courageous Italian defence in the grim mountains of Eritrea and Ethiopia where British battalions were serving with two Indian Army divisions. In the eleven day March 1941 Battle of Keren the boulder-strewn mountain slopes were too difficult even for mules. Food supplies were dropped from the air by two elderly R.A.F. aircraft but even for this soldiers had to drag consignments packed in sandbags and two gallon tins of water up the steep slopes in sweltering heat, sometimes over 50 degrees. Under fire the drops of food and water were limited to two a day, leaving the soldiers with but one pint of water per day.

The British and Commonwealth forces' stay in Greece and Crete was valiant, uncomfortable due to extremes of climate, difficult due to mountainous terrain, especially on the Greek mainland, and short. Food at best was bully beef and biscuit with virtually no supplies available locally, often there were days with half rations and some with none. Thirst after long withdrawal marches was a permanent hardship, there being few wells in towns and villages. In Crete there was an added and unusual irritant, the hurried withdrawal to the island had left cooking stoves and utensils, even mess-tins behind on the mainland, so making preparation and distribution of food difficult. Again, many soldiers' first meal was aboard a Royal Navy warship taking them, at great risk and several losses of ships, to the safety of Alexandria.

Overall, in these first three years of the war the Army in the Middle East had made a great effort to improve the standards of soldiers' food reflecting the general improvement throughout the Army. Nevertheless, some regiments still retained poor cooks with little imagination, content to accordingly produce only monotony. And as always, battlefield conditions could negate the work of even the best field cooks. And, very wisely, the United Kingdom Government in 1941 took steps to acquire the entire available world production of tea.

6

The Second World War: 1942–1945

The last years of the war included the major campaigns in Tunisia, Sicily, Italy and North West Europe, with in the war against Japan the brief and disastrous campaign in Malaya, the long major campaigns in Burma and one minor but important operation in Madagascar. For feeding the frontline soldiers in all the major campaigns compo rations were introduced at different times and speeds.

In the early months of the war research into the possibility for compo rations had been in progress, the brief campaign in Norway had highlighted the value. The aims of compo were to limit to as few as possible the occasions when a soldier had to put up with bully beef and biscuits, to include Vitamin D in the form of fruit and vegetables in the soldier's daily ration, and to keep the soldiers well fed with a variety of food that they would like until such time as the March 1941 field service ration scale provisions were available and could be cooked in the field. And, as important as any dietary factor was that boxes of compo tins and later weather-proof cartons could be designed to fit together, taking minimum space in lorries. Finally compo for the individual soldier by D-Day came to include not the least of its blessings, hexamine tablets (solid fuel in tablet form) and a little metal burner stand, meaning the soldier could heat food or even just make a mess tin of hot tea quickly simply and with care not exhibiting a give-away light, always provided, of course that the limited supply of hexamine tablets had not run out, and that his matches had remained dry.

Development of the compo rations owed much to the expert advice of pre-war Polar explorers, many of whom, including Quintin Riley, joined the commandos. First was a very basic 48 hour pack for a single soldier including little mini-tins of tea, sugar, powdered milk, cheese, biscuits and cigarettes with a light-weight version of the Tommy cooker. An improved 24 hour version including compressed meat and oatmeal and tea and sugar blocks together with biscuits and cigarettes packed in waterproof covering was produced for soldiers in the North African landings of November 1942, followed by the inclusion of salt and chewing-gum to aid saliva. By the end of the year the classic fourteen-man packs were on their way to North Africa. The ration for each man was intended to provide a filling breakfast and evening meal with a light snack at midday and chocolates and sweets for periods on the march. As it was appreciated that no two soldiers would ever agree on what compo packs should contain but would exchange to suit each other's taste, the containers came in seven varieties, six in each of the fourteen-man packs. Among the dishes were steak and kidney, haricot oxtails, meat and vegetables, luncheon meat, stewed steak, red salmon, rice pudding, fruit pudding, treacle pudding, sweets, chewing-gum and cigarettes. Cooking, however, at first still remained by Tommy cookers.

Compo revolutionised the feeding of the front-line soldier and has remained the basis of British Army feeding ever since. As a food foundation, however, it had and continues to have three weaknesses, not always perceived and understood. On occasions it has led commanders to overlook the importance of the provision of supplementary fresh food, especially fruit and vegetables, with some unfortunate results. Compo can also produce a condition now known to many civilian families. Although appearing in half a dozen varieties, just as supermarket age families were later to experience, a 'monotony of the six varieties' could sometimes set in, particularly over a long period and if no fresh produce was available more became very quickly affected. Thirdly, before long compo stocks accumulated, leaving staffs with a feeling that in the interests of economy that they should be 'turned over'. Initial ration supplies to a particular campaign often therefore included compo rations not well suited to the terrain and climate of the new campaign territory.

Special compo ration packs were designed for tank crews of three or four men and for commando Arctic operations. These latter were at a 5,000 calories per day level, pemmican replacing meat and including ascorbic acid tablets, and with an oil pressure stove replacing the Tommy cooker.

Algeria and Tunisia 1942-45

British and American forces landed from the sea in Morocco and Algeria on 8 November 1942. Later, joined by a French army contingent, they began a move eastward, often under heavy German air attack towards and later into Tunisia. Almost immediately after the Allied landings substantial German forces arrived in Tunisia to join the remainder of the Afrika Korps, while on 16 February the Eighth Army entered Tunisia from the south. Clearing the Germans and Italians out of

Tunisia therefore involved some very stiff fighting in mountainous territory, mud, and in the winter very cold weather. Success was to follow when German resistance ended on 13 May 1943. The British First Army that had landed in Algeria was more suitably equipped but lacked the Eighth Army's battle experience. It was also the first large force to be issued with the new compo rations in 24 hour packs of fourteen—food for fourteen men for one day or for one man for fourteen days. These formed the diet of the two First Army divisions and others landed in the initial six weeks. Eggs were also available locally to add variety and were quick to boil for men in a hurry. Thereafter normal field service ration foodstuffs arrived from England; bread was baked locally and refrigeration facilities were at work in Algiers. Eighth Army men who had lived on the desert scale ration bully beef, biscuits, tea and lime juice were a little sniffy about the First Army's greatly superior compo rations; such comments as "All right for some" and "Luxury food" could be heard.

The compo fourteen-man packs were certainly found easier to convey, but transport remained a problem. The light wooden packaging of the packs was easily damaged and pillaging became a nuisance with widespread stealing of food. During the winter months mud made the roads in Tunisia's mountain areas impossible for lorries and mules were used to supply forward formations and units.

Sicily and Italy 1943-45

After the ejection of the Germans from North Africa there followed the next logical step for the Mediterranean theatre, the invasion first of Sicily and then of the Italian mainland despite the increasing priority for Allied resources going to the preparations for D-Day. The campaign in Sicily opened on the 10 July 1943 and lasted a month. The twenty-one month campaign in Italy began with landings in South Italy on 9 September with fighting to continue until the end of the war in May 1945. In Sicily British troops landing from the sea (including to their disgust some men from the Parachute Regiment), all carried two 24 hour ration packs with them. Thereafter regiments lived on compo rations until 28 July when normal field ration scale food preparation was feasible, supplemented by local fruit and vegetable produce and, for the fortunate, Sicilian wine. Initially bread baked in Malta was provided, later field bakeries were set up. However, difficulties in the Mount Etna area foreshadowed the huge problems to follow later on the mainland and frontline units were returned to basic compo with neither bread nor fresh meat. For this area locally requisitioned mules of very varying quality had to be

A soldier of the Green Howards eating a salmon sandwich outside his Anzio beachhead dug-out. (Regimental museum of the Green Howards)

used, the animals suffering severely from totally inexperienced drivers. The Anglo-American campaign ended on 17 August.

After a preparatory hot meal British troops were the first to land in Calabria, the 'toe' of Italy on 3 September. Other American and British landings followed almost simultaneously. Initial resistance was weak until German reinforcements arrived, and at first emergency rations and a little later compo could be well supplemented by local fruit and vegetables. Further inland and up the peninsula was soon to see an increasingly hard fought autumn and winter campaign, troops from both armies slowly moving up the Italian peninsula. This advance was supported by a British and American landing at Salerno on 9 September which, after stiff combat, linked up with the main force advancing from the south on the 16th. A stalemate then followed. A second Allied landing from the sea at Anzio followed on 22 January 1944 and after four months of further heavy fighting finally linked up with the American forces advancing from the south. The way to the Italian capital was now open. After the entry into Rome on 5 June 1944 the Allied troops continued their slow, hard-fought way up the Italian peninsula, enduring a second winter and occupying Venice and Milan by the time of the German surrender. Throughout the whole campaign the Germans were exceptionally well-fed and fought in a series of defensive lines with great resolution.

The terrain of mainland Italy presented particularly difficult problems for an army trying to advance, problems both of tactics and of supply, even from the start mules being indispensable. While the first landings in the south had met weak opposition, those at Salerno and Anzio had initially to gain control of flat sand, dune or marshy open land with little more than scrub bushes to provide cover against fire from quickly but well prepared German defence positions. At Anzio winter rain and cold added to the difficulties. A little way inland the Allied regiments found themselves in what they described as 'wadi' country, hills, narrow tracks and paths, and ravines that quickly became squelching mud up to knee level after heavy rain. Soldiers in both landings were fed a hot meal on board the landing ships but had to remain on a waterproof ration pack including tea, biscuits, two blocks of oatmeal and one of compressed meat, three slabs of chocolate (two of raisin and one plain), packets of two pints worth of tea including milk and sugar blocks, salt and chewing-gum. This was supplemented as soon as possible by very traditional bully beef and biscuits during the first two or three days. At Salerno rum and compo rations followed for the next eight days of grim fighting. At Anzio the Allied and German positions were on some occasions less than fifty yards apart. Allied soldiers not able even to have a tin of hot tea had to listen to the Germans preparing their food. For the British food was initially back to Maconochie's stew or even sandwiches together with two mess tins of water per day. Imagination again created new ideas, the most remarkable perhaps being the use by at least one regiment of liver salts as a baking powder, Eno's and Andrews producing good light pastry in the absence of flour. When the beach perimeters were enlarged and secured patterns were developed of half compo and half field service ration scales, these later changed to full field service scales with fresh bread when conditions so permitted.

Regiments advancing up the Italian peninsula following the initial Calabria landings had to face the 'spine' of the peninsula, grey, barren, mountainous in places so steep that in the snow neither jeeps nor even mules could bring up food rations and Indian porters had to be used. In the higher mountain regions there was generally no very clear immediate front, combat was a matter of scattered foxholes and scrapes, often filled with large beetles, facing strong mutually supporting German fire position defences. While in the spring, summer and early autumn months local meat, fruit and vegetables were often to hand, and roads permitting mobile bakeries were sent forward, in the winter regiments were lucky if they could find a few sheep or goats. Food prepared on petrol cookers had often to be limited to bully beef, Maconochies, biscuits and tea at best, in 48 hour packs prior to an attack. Many of the difficulties also faced the Germans and sometimes in the winter a simultaneous mutual clanging of mess tins gained a brief ceasefire; at other times though the severity of the fighting meant that food might not be delivered for one or two days.

Before the capture of Rome the advance from the south had been halted by the crucial long battle of Monte Cassino where the surrounding region was dominated by a massive system of mountain tops and ridges. The Benedictine Cassino monastery, at 5,000 feet, and now converted into a fortress, towered over and directed artillery fire onto the ground below. As they approached Cassino food supply, jeep to mule, mule to units, perhaps a six mile journey for between sixty and a hundred mules for each battalion, all had to be made at night, and as quickly and quietly as possible. Many of the mule drivers were expert Basutos from southern Africa and some of the mules in packs had to be dyed to a darker protective colour. The food was then cooked in rear reserve company positions or a regimental headquarters during the following afternoon, and then at dusk carried onward by the Indian porters to the forward detachments, arriving after nightfall. To preserve warmth meat was often incorporated into pies and pasties. These were then wrapped in straw or newspaper along with a flask of water for tea stuffed in the porters' sandbags. Although often tepid on arrival the food was very welcome for men freezing in the mountain cold. When the food arrived men crawled or crept out of their holes at around 11.00 p.m., but until the next evening they would be lucky if they could just get a mess-tin of tea. The military operation plan was to try to prise the Germans out of their numerous mountainside defence positions; for soldiers waiting or preparing for a local attack this meant living by day head down or lying flat in a shell hole or a digging, surrounded by decomposing corpses or mules and under periodic heavy bombardment. Before an attack men in a battalion brought to the front to lead the operation would be given a small 24 hour ration pack - bully beef, chocolate, biscuits, tea and a hexamine burner.

The final week-long attack ending on 18 May set the pattern of operations against further strongly defended German fortified lines for the rest of the Italian campaign. Units were given a period of rest before attacks and a hot meal immediately preceding them. At other times rations alternated between the compo cooked breakfast, midday snack and evening meal, unless the fighting was intense when soldiers were at best provided with food in vacuum flasks, or more often found themselves back to bully beef, biscuits and tea. In the summer and autumn plenty of local fruit and vegetables and some meat were again available as well as wine. In the July heat thirst became acute for men on the march who generally preferred to retain their water bottles full until the evening as the water bowsers often arrived late. They would suck pebbles or chew gum on the march, "Our thirst would be worth a fortune to a brewery" remarked one soldier.

The Italian campaign was as testing as any in the war.

North-West Europe 1944-45

The most careful preparations were made to ensure that the 21st Army Group troops landing in Normandy on D-Day, 6 June 1944, had been well trained and well fed in the preceding weeks. On their way, both in south England and on the landing craft, tea or hot snack food were provided. Each soldier, seasick and already weary, splashing ashore on the Normandy beaches carried with him two 24 hour compo ration packs. Each of these packs contained, in a weather-proof cardboard box measuring 6" x 5" x 2 ½", a small dinner hard 'brick' of meat and vegetable stew, and a second breakfast 'brick' of porridge, these melted down and heated in water provided solid hot meals. Also in the box were small blocks of compressed tea with milk and sugar, a few soft unsweetened biscuits, a block of meat extract, chocolate, boiled sweets, chewing-gum, lump sugar and salt. In addition to the two boxes each soldier carried a small tin of bully beef and two water bottles.

Even before the beaches were secured men from the newly formed Army Catering Corps were landing under fire in the first line transport of the formations and units they were tasked to support. These sections equipped with portable petrol cookers, quickly set to work in farm buildings or in trenches. When possible soldiers' compo rations were pooled for units and sub-units in feeding points; in the immediate front line soldiers were released from their company and platoon positions or duties two at a time to their sub-unit 'cooker's' location to eat, or food

Soldiers of 107 Regiment Royal Armoured Corps (King's Own) alongside Churchill tanks, North-West Europe 1944-45. (Regimental museum, King's Own Royal Regiment)

would be taken, often under fire, and usually by sergeants, from these locations to the forward trenches or in vehicles in thermos heated hay boxes. When the beachheads became large enough rest centre areas well supplied with food and spread over two or three villages were opened up for units which had been given a day or more's rest.

After the breakthrough in July the 21st Army Group divisions moved swiftly through north-west France, Belgium and Holland, reaching the frontiers of Germany in December, on occasions food supplies being dropped from aircraft. On the move in France local meat, fruit and vegetables were given by or could be bought from the local French populace usually with good will, but also some resentment over the destruction of Caen; in Belgium and Holland what was available was bought or given freely; in Germany food was taken without any explanation being thought necessary. In Belgium also the opportunity was taken to purchase the products of three Belgian bacon factories which could replace the unpopular compo soya-based sausage in emergency packs. With units on the move, the brief halts for a brew up of tea remained all-important.

The ill-judged airborne landing at Arnhem in September 1944 and the long battle that followed exhausted the ration packs carried by soldiers. Many had to remain for over a week on rations designed for two days. For the more fortunate a local bakery was utilised for several days, the chickens, rabbits and a goat of a local farm and food found in houses all came to be used. The airborne regiments' fighting was epic but among the many lessons to be learnt was that of supply for a force projected too far.

By the end of 1944 further valuable experience had been learnt and put to good use. Transport and operational conditions permitting, some of the dehydrated packed foods given to the civil population in Britain could be sent up with the rations—cabbage, carrots and potatoes and then eggs, meat, Spam and more varied vegetables. Fishmeal, useful for preparing fish dishes, followed. For cooking the No 1 Cooker was modified, becoming more efficient, for field improvised cooking a fuel composed of waste oil, water and sawdust was again found to be useful. The compo packs could now be varied in size, for two, seven or fourteen men, this larger one feeding fourteen men for 24 hours or seven men for 48 hours. Packs for airborne and special forces were developed. It was found that ten of the D-Day landing one-day packs could keep a soldier in efficient condition for ten days, and a variety of special packs for different conditions and theatres followed. Perhaps simply the most important development though was the introduction of hexamine tablet burner, enabling the individual soldier in his trench or foxhole to cook his own meals and eat them from his mess-tin, or in the cold of the 1944-45 winter at least give him a mess-tin full of hot tea. The burner was almost odourless and its inconspicuous flame, easy to conceal if not in a vehicle or at least behind cover, provided a reassuring warming glow as well as its use as a cooker. Conditions had also greatly improved for armoured vehicle crews, special metal boxes being fitted in tanks to carry a pack of three days' reserve for the crews, including preserved meat, sardines, canned beans, biscuits, margarine, sugar, jam and tea.

Difficulties, however, remained. In flat open country soldiers carrying hay boxes to forward detachments presented a target, food had to be carried at nights and taking longer no longer arrived hot. The battlefield could not always permit two meals per day. In close combat soldiers would be back to 48 hour emergency rations, soya link sausages between thick slices of bread or tinned meat and biscuits, together with tea. If a unit's stock of hexamine ran out and fighting was intense food would have to be eaten cold, as happened frequently in the 1944-45 winter operations in Holland and Germany. In some sectors the oil drum filled with sand and petrol, the 'Benghazi Burner', was used again. For a number of regiments, although by no means all, self-heating tins of tomato soup began to appear, the tins including a wick that could be lit from a cigarette. Before an attack, however, soldiers were usually provided with a hot meal based on proper cooking of compo rations or dehydrated foods sent up with the rations, supplemented by anything acquired locally.

No scruples were had by units entering the rich German farmland where meat of all varieties, beef, lamb, bacon, chicken, duck, goat and eggs together with milk, sometimes butter, potatoes and vegetables were taken from households and farmsteads and cooked and eaten in kitchens and barns. Accounts of these last months of the campaign are full of tales of the relish with which cold and battle weary soldiers enjoyed these homely changes from the ration issues, and of the great effect on morale and resolution.

Less pleasant, however, are the accounts of drink - German beer, wines and spirits were also seen as the victors' spoils. On a number of occasions small groups of men, sections or platoons, would come across a well-stocked shop or house and incapacitate themselves to the horror of their officers; in fairness, fortunately these occasions were usually in phases of the battle when the soldiers concerned were not in immediate direct contact with their enemies. The temptation was strong for men who had been in battle for several months and had seen friends wounded and killed, tensions sought relief.

The German surrender ended the largest scale military operations conducted by the British Army in the Second World War, from Normandy to the crossing of the Rhine with hard fighting. Each regiment or battalion had, as part of its own 'cap badge' establishment, its quartermaster, quartermaster-sergeants and platoon sergeants proud of their roles, sparing no effort to ensure their men's food supply, and as much in danger of an enemy air attack or artillery bombardment as anyone else in the regiment. They were referred to with no disrespect whatever, as the L.O.B. 'Left out of Battle'. Certainly no term could have been more misleading, "Thank You, Q" was the almost universal view at the regimental or company cookers.

The War against Japan: Malaya and Madagascar 1941-42

The well-prepared Japanese landings on the Malay Peninsula, beginning on the day after Pearl Harbor, 8 December, opened a campaign in which British, Indian, Australian and Malay units were unable to stop the Japanese Army, far superior both in numbers and in training. The British defence plan had anticipated Japanese landings in the north and pre-positioned dumps of preserved and tinned food had been prepared for defending regiments. These dumps were very quickly overrun by the Japanese, but others further south that had not been able to reach the north in time kept units reasonably well fed, and so they were able, after hard fighting, to withdraw to Singapore Island. There bakeries and cold storage facilities kept the defenders fed initially, but Japanese landings on the east coast of the island soon deprived the garrison of almost all food. Air attacks and shortage of dock labourers prevented supplies being shipped in. On 15 February the ceasefire was ordered—for the remaining members of the garrison to usher in three and a half years of hunger, suffering and for many death.

The huge French island colony of Madagascar had remained under the control of authorities loyal to the Vichy regime after the Fall of France. The entry of Japan into the war posed the likelihood of the Japanese Navy wishing to use facilities on the island, and also highlighted the possible value of the island for the Royal Navy. The Vichy colonial administration refused any suggestion of co-operation and a military and naval force occupied the chief port Diego Suarez, in the north, after a brief three-day combat in early May 1942. A full-scale military operation to take control over the whole island and involving one British and four African colonial brigades was mounted later on 10 September. In May it had been estimated that in this operation it would be necessary to keep the British forces on bully beef and biscuits for sixty days. In the event and after a few days of local fighting in May and the rather longer six weeks period of fighting in September and October Madagascar became a fighting soldier's 'Garden of Eden'. The local meat canning industry provided fresh and tinned meat, locally baked bread was available six days after the May landings and after the indigenous population had, area by area, recovered from panic flights into the bush, men came out to offer fresh fruit and vegetables for sale. Compo rations were withdrawn seven days after the September landings—to the relief of soldiers who had not enjoyed the melting of chocolate, cheese and dripping in the hot sun. After further fighting the campaign from which the British Army units were withdrawn in mid-October, finally ended on 6 November.

The War against Japan: Burma 1941-45

The long Burma campaign was of especial difficulty - other theatres having priority it was seriously undersupplied for long periods until 1945. The tropical jungle conditions combined with frequent inadequate rations lowering body resistance created major health problems, in particular malaria and scrub typhus but also fever, sores, insect bites and the sheer exhaustion and fatigue exacerbated by the jungle, heat and mountains. Rainfall, in particular the monsoon season from May to September, brought much transport to a standstill and kept soldiers in wet uniforms for long periods. In a few areas there were plains and fruit groves, but for most soldiers Burma was evil-smelling jungle, thick undergrowth and mud slopes sometimes reducing soldier movement on to hands and knees. Tactically the jungle badly limited visibility, a view from a hill summit might be one only of the tops of trees. At the outset of the campaign the Japanese were superior in these conditions, and time was needed for the British and Indian Armies to regain mastery. The terrain and the size of the country made anything approaching a front line impossible, engagements small or large scale centred on attacking or defending particular areas of local tactical importance. The shortage of vehicles meant that men had to march in most weathers while mule trains, up to one hundred per battalion, followed with food, ammunition and tents until all-weather air supply could be provided. Mules also had the useful advantage of being able to swim across rivers while carrying their loads. In the Arakan Mountain area where air drops were often not feasible mules were indispensable, but sometimes the terrain was so difficult that rations had to be abandoned. In these conditions food supply varied greatly according to area, weather and battlefield conditions, an overall uniformity was never possible and accounts based on particular examples paint the clearest picture. For the campaign itself the year 1942 saw the Japanese overrunning Burma and pushing the Fourteenth Army a little way across the frontier into India; increasingly exhausted they failed to make any serious progress in the following year. An ill-judged desperate attempt in March 1944 ended in disaster for the Japanese at Imphal and at Kohima where a sixteen-day siege of the British garrison failed. British forces opened their major operation to evict the Japanese from Burma in November-December 1944, progressively clearing the Japanese from Upper Burma, and after linking with forces from west of the Arakan range that had been landed from the sea, occupied Rangoon on 2 May 1945. As the campaign progressed, more and more aircraft became available for use in dropping food supplies. Although monsoon weather could prevent aircraft being used for long periods, air supply was a major factor in victory.

A Chindit and mule, 211 Column, 2nd Battalion the King's Own Royal Regiment, April 1944. The cardboard boxes to the soldier's right contain American K rations. Behind him is one of the tin boxes containing a seven day ration pack. (Regimental museum, King's Own Royal Regiment)

Food for the British soldier became simply what was to hand or possible at any one time, generally far from the official 1942 scale of tinned meat, usually bully beef, and vegetables, dried fruit, biscuits, tea, condensed milk and sugar all in a 24 hour waterproof pack. This pack was replaced in 1945 by a new 'Pacific' 24 hour pack of low weight and high nutrition comprising packaged ham and an egg, a midday chocolate or other biscuit snack, tea and an evening ham and beef pack meal. Attempts in 1943 to bring fresh meat to India largely failed, the journey being too long. Frozen mutton from Australia in 1944 was more successful, conditions permitting reaching soldiers three times a week. Heating and cooking was generally mess-tins over Tommy cookers or small fires of bamboo, in static periods regimental and company cookers could be set up. In small section outposts tea would be brewed up over a punctured biscuit tin or compo tin burner with a handle made of signal wire and strained through a mosquito net or someone's sock. The tea leaves would then be dried, soaked in rum and used as tobacco. Water was a problem throughout the campaign, local water being exceedingly dangerous to drink unless purified by tablets issued and carried by all soldiers. The worst danger from polluted water was leptospirosis, a life-threatening disease of the kidneys. At Imphal a rough and ready airstrip enabled some food to be flown in, supplies were also dropped by air, some consignments were parachuted, a locally made 'parajute' being used, others were dropped with varying accuracy in boxes. In Kohima the dangers from Japanese snipers made it necessary for regimental non-commissioned officers to crawl forward in the cold mud and darkness of night, pushing big dishes of stew and dehydrated potatoes mixed with margarine towards soldiers in slit trenches. There mess-tins would appear above ground level, two per man one for stew and one for two mouthfuls of water for tea, if the soldiers still had tea packets, if not tea itself. Both stew and water were no longer hot by the time the last trench was reached. Cooking fires were not allowed, their smoke being a give-away, but at least one unit dug a deep trench, covered it with branches and lit a fire at dusk when the smoke would not be conspicuous. By the last days of the siege at Kohima soldiers were reduced to half a tin of bully beef with perhaps for some a small tin of pilchards, five biscuits, small portions of butter, tinned cheese and jam and tea limited to the half pint ration of water per day. The terrain at Kohima was so difficult that no airstrip was possible and all supplies had to be dropped.

Bully beef, as always in the tropical heat, became soft and greasy and the stew made from it was known as 'burgoo', the term was also applied to a porridge made of meat and crushed biscuits. Quality varied, the poorest were held by soldiers to been made from mule meat into which some of their harnesses had slipped. Another very unpopular form of meat was soya-link sausages. Occasionally local meat could be acquired, usually goat. In some areas at the correct season local fruit such as mangoes and bananas, vegetables such as beans, cucumbers and pumpkins, together with eggs could be bought or bartered. On some occasions American 'K' rations were issued, for breakfast an unpleasant form of bacon and scrambled egg hash, a candy or stale chocolate bar with nuts, a few U.S. Camel brand cigarettes, a few small biscuits and a coffee block. There followed a midday snack of biscuits and cheese spread, synthetic lemon juice and coffee with a supper of soup powder, meat loaf, biscuits and chocolate. These rations were not at all popular, especially the coffee, the British soldier missing his tea. At fortunate times field kitchens could be set up behind a regiment defending a particular area and two good and varied meals and a snack from U.K.-produced compo packs. At other times when monsoon rain limited or prevented air drops soldiers could be on half basic rations for over a month. Air drops could lead to pillaging, soldiers from one unit scavenging in a drop prepared for another unit or helping themselves from boxes that had been broken open on hitting the ground. Food was generally issued and eaten at night or very early in the morning.

The 'Chindit' Long Range Penetration regiments had to experience all the supply problems that faced big but lightly equipped formations moving very far forward or deep behind the enemy's front line. The Chindit Commander, Brigadier Orde Wingate, whose temperament at times was unbalanced, held a puritanical military fundamentalist view which he expressed openly, that hardship was an indispensible moral fibre part of Long Range Penetration. For his first 1943 Chindit operation of one brigade size (including one British battalion) he opted for rations designed for a two day parachute assault, twelve ounces of biscuits, two ounces of cheese, one ounce of powdered milk, nine ounces of packed almonds or raisins, an ounce of sweets, three quarters of an ounce of tea, four ounces of sugar, a small folder of salt and twenty cigarettes. This ration contained no meat and little protein, at best 2,800 calories per day. Soldiers were expected to carry five days' rations with them on the march. Wingate claimed that air supply would assist but in 1943 there were very few transport aircraft; he also added that game could be shot on the march - hardly realistic for columns supposed to be on secret penetration. On the long marches men fell ill, a number dying, almost all lost efficiency. For his second very much larger, six brigade size (including fourteen British battalions) Chindit operation in 1944 Wingate opted for the American lightweight 'K' ration, a taste not shared by many of his followers, monotonous and varying between 2,800 and 3,200 calories per day, some way short of the 4,000 minimum necessary for twelve to fifteen weeks of strenuous tropical operations. In the event units often ran out of rations and for several reasons could not be resupplied immediately. For one column of the King's Own Royal Regiment that had no food for four and a half days and no water for two the battalion chaplain distributed Communion wafers and wine, seeing it as a Christian duty. The soldiers were recorded as being 'pathetically grateful'. In the course of the operation the columns were forced to fight as normal infantry and became very dependent on air supply when this was feasible. Air supply took the form of hurriedly constructed airstrips, parachute drops and supply gliders. Mules were flown in for onward food distribution, apparently raising only moderate objections in aircraft or gliders. The hapless animals were 'devocalised', their vocal chords cut so that they would make no noise giving away a position; some were dyed with a mix of potassium permanganate and coffee grounds as camouflage. Inadequate food - in the daunting words of one staff officer "undue hunger" - played a large part in the limited success of Chindit operations, and a special rehabilitation ration scale was authorised for survivors.

By 1945 improved foods, much from New Zealand including tinned meat, bacon, fruit, vegetables and baskets of eggs, were arriving and could be distributed to units near an emergency airstrip or by drop. Cigarettes were generally but not always in good supply and some of very poor quality, the best were sent from volunteer organisations in the United Kingdom to their local county regiments. There was a rum issue at times of intense fighting and on occasions a few bottles of beer appeared.

One Scots regiment actually used food as a field punishment for disciplinary offences. The miscreant would be required to sit next to his Company Sergeant Major while he was cooking his food or brewing his tea or coffee.

Overall, however, the soldier in Burma had to put up with the worst food and most difficult conditions of any British soldiers in any theatre of the war. The daily calorie value even for those not in Chindit columns fell well below the 4,000 needed for efficiency, in some cases, not only in the Chindits, below 3,000. Many soldiers returned home with their health undermined for life despite all the best efforts of staffs, airmen, muleteers and vehicle drivers.

7

The Post-War Years 1945–1965

In the first post-1945 decades the British Army found itself engaged in three types of operations. The largest scale type of operation was against the formal, sometimes, uniformed army of an enemy and included the Korean War of 1950 to 1953, the Suez operation of 1956 and the Borneo campaign of 1962 to 1967 which was fought in jungle conditions. Also involving many regiments was a series of major 'end of empire' counter-insurgency campaigns in Palestine, Malaya, Kenya, Cyprus and Aden, with several smaller police actions in a number of other territories. In both of these types the provision of food to the soldier in the frontline or out on patrol in some campaigns created problems. Compo appeared initially in a 'one pack fits all theatres' distribution of leftover wartime stocks. Wise regiments had to use their messing cash component to supplement compo, wherever possible, with low cost nutritional items such as flour to make pastry for pies, eggs, rice, sugar, curry powder and any local vegetables obtainable to make food more acceptable. This applied as much also to the third type of operation, to continue until the early 1990s, which was the maintenance of an army in western Germany as part of the North Atlantic Treaty Organisation's (NATO) defences against any attack by the Soviet-controlled Warsaw Pact forces in Eastern Germany. Happily in this field no combat took place and British Army of the Rhine (B.A.O.R.) exercises, although testing, do not form part of this work. The Army itself remained conscript until 1960-62, thereafter it had to compete in the market for recruits with consequential improving of the standards of rations. The Army Catering Corps, which some had planned to disband, survived and continued to develop more imaginative rations and cooking. In 1993, however, the Corps became incorporated in the new Royal Logistic Corps.

Counter-Insurgency 1948-67

Major campaigns were fought by the British Army after the end of the Second World War and the first of the major counter-insurgency campaigns was in Palestine. In many respects fighting had begun even before the German war had ended with Jewish nationalists staking out their claim for the future state of Israel. The Jews turned to an atmosphere of bitter vicious hatred against the British Army. The campaign became one of several Jewish terror groups attacking the garrison of three divisions of British troops and administration centres, with later attacks on the Arab community. Most of the work of the British regiments was initially reactive, the protection of centres, port, railway and road communications, oil installations and military posts against constant sabotage attempts, together with urban cordon and search operations. The food supply to troops engaged was never a serious problem, so much of the military work being mounted from base camps in or near urban areas. Regiment and company level headquarters were able to provide cooked compo based food by rotation of detachments; in major proactive cordon and search operations. Second World War emergency 48 hour packs were issued.

The campaign in Malaya, opening in 1948 and continuing until 1960, was the longest and most important of the colonial counter-insurgency conflicts. It was occasioned by a terrorist guerrilla movement, Communist in ideology and largely but not entirely drawn from the Malay peninusla's Chinese minority. At the outset the uprising involved five British battalions, at its peak twelve, together with other British units and an equal number of battalions from other Commonwealth countries. From 1952 to 1954 the administration and military were led by the British Army's outstanding post-1945 General, Sir Gerald Templer.

The terrain presented many of the tactical and supply difficulties of those in Burma - very dense jungle, hills, streams, besides rubber plantations that had to be secured; animals, leeches, mosquitoes and heat that affected soldiers until mastered after training; and an insurgency force numbering 8,000 at its peak, that knew the country well and how to live and fight in it.

Despite the experience of Burma, the Army had to enter a learning curve. Battalions had a few officers and sergeants with jungle know-how, and were now composed of young 18-21 year old subaltern officers and soldiers, mostly town-dwellers, recently conscripted and hurriedly trained. The first operations were cautious, preoccupied with security of the administration and plantations. Strategy then became proactive, in the jungle based on platoon bivouac positions linked in a battalion of brigade pattern in order to control an area. Each platoon would send

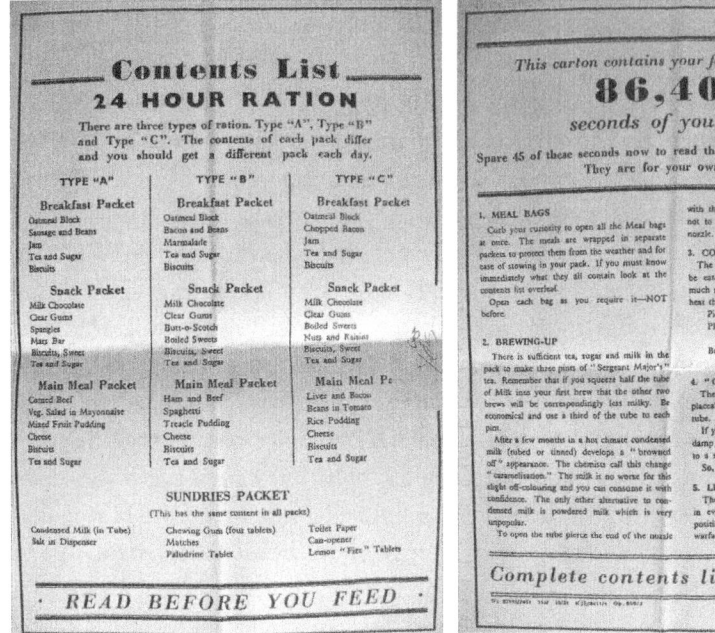

Rations issued in Malaya to an infantry battalion. (Queen's Own Royal West Kent Regiment archives)

out two ten-men patrols for ambush, tracking and pursuit, or food (rice), denial village search work. With experience the platoons were directed to extend their activities from a single day to three frequently to five and then ten days. A few were extended to four weeks in particular circumstances. Patrols became bigger, up to thirty men, mounting round the clock ambushes on a watch and rest rota. Basic to the original platoon patrol concept came the ten-man ration pack and the 5lb weight of the individual ration that the soldier could be expected to carry with all his other equipment in the heat and jungle conditions. At the outset, in 1948-49, patrols out for a day or two carried little more than a bag of rice and dates, or if for a few days tins of bully beef and biscuits. There were no ration packs and no air drops at this time. Later when patrols were out for longer periods additional supply came to be provided by the unit—supply escorted against guerrillas by the regiment's bandsmen until the number of military bands was reduced, or dropped from the air. The patrols themselves were sent out from unit bases or company detachment bases where field cookers provided full meals for soldiers preparing to go out on patrol or returning in varying degrees of exhaustion. Cooking was done on stoves with double-jacket boilers fuelled by wood purchased locally, or on No 1 Cookers fuelled by petrol. These bases would include a NAAFI facility with beer.

Supply to units was generally by vehicle, though these were sometimes attacked while on the road. In the 1950s aircraft and later helicopters began to supply forward patrols. One or two regiments in deep jungle were supplied by elephants. Regiments were issued with either British, or the rather more generous Australian packs, these contained a slightly greater allowance of meat and bread and did not include the unpopular fish option in the British compo packs. Platoon sergeants conveyed a rum issue in one of their water bottles and all soldiers received fifty free cigarettes per week. From 1949 onwards regimental and company level bases provided three varieties of 24 hour rations in ten-man packs which were prepared and cooked on the site or taken into an ambush or other tactical operation. There, particularly if big patrols were to be out for several days, food might be heated, but it often had to be eaten cold. The leaflet issued to soldiers, in this case men of the Royal West Kent Regiment, describes the food (see image).

In 1952 experiments for a new jungle compo ration began; later in 1959 this resulted in the 24 hour daily ration pack of a lighter breakfast without bacon, beans or sausage, but retaining the midday snack and the main evening meal for which six varieties were available. A two day pack load for thirty men, however, would not always offer all six. The most important new addition was lemonade powder and the provision of eating rather than cooking chocolate; both were very well received. By 1953-54 Army Catering Corps cooks, usually cook sergeants at unit headquarters and corporals and cooks to companies, were attached to regiments. On active operations breakfast was usually very early, 2.00 a.m. and the evening meal at 8.00 p.m. or later, cooking being done in darkness.

An Army bakery was set up and contracts with local suppliers for additional tea, butter, margarine and tinned meats were made. Fruit, pineapples and bananas, local fish, eggs and a variety of vegetables were also available. Two of these, though were only a limited success, the fish being very bony and requiring filleting before cooking, and the eggs having a greenish yolk, emitting an unpleasant smell and erupting when fried. Local indigenous petty entrepreneurs also offered their services. A Mr Alf Gull claiming on an advertisement to be by appointment to 'many chota and burrah sahibs' offered 'Pukka Blighty Charwallah early morning tea' a speciality at Paroi Camp, Seremban. At Jemaluang Camp a 'McGregor Pukka Clued-Up Blighty Charwalla by Special Appointment to the Admiral of Johore' offered egg banjo (on credit), tea and chips, proudly displaying a motto "Not to Worry Mucker, I bring it complete tomorrow". Business appears to have been brisk. The 1st Queen's Royal Regiment captured an entire insurgent food dump and used some of the contents.

The campaign in Malaya became the template for other British colonial counter-insurgency operations, the strategy, tactics and supply procedures becoming the model for the three campaigns that followed. In mainly but not entirely all infantry operations patrols led by junior officers, sergeants and corporals would be sent out from regiments or company headquarters, the patrols living on lightweight short-term rations with more substantial cooked food being supplied at base headquarters.

In the campaign against the Mau Mau insurrection in Kenya, initially one but very soon after a further four British battalions together with five or six African units were deployed. The campaign lasted from 1952 until 1956. The British battalions were at first tasked with security in Nairobi and the white settled areas where farmers were generous with food and drink to such an extent that the Army had to issue cautions over excess hospitality. However, regiments were soon sent into the rainforest, bamboo forest and alpine moor areas of the Aberdares and Mount Kenya, 8,000 to 10,000 feet in altitude. These operations took the form of either several company or battalion big sweeps of a particular area, or patrols to ambush or pursue insurgent groups. These groups became increasingly adept at survival. Patrols operated from company bases where compo rations were cooked on No 1 Cookers, and bivouacs provided rest. Local fruit, vegetables and fish could often be brought forward to the company bases. Between ten and fifteen men strong patrols would be sent out for twenty-four to seventy-two hours in the forest, their food was compo to be eaten cold, speech limited to a whisper. The big sweeps could take a company into the forest for up to a fortnight when food supplies would be dropped by the light aircraft of the Kenya Police Reserve Air Wing; the drops, usually in 30lb sacks, were made from aircraft flying at very low level. The altitude of the forests and the dangers from animals, in particular rhinoceros, elephant and buffalo, some crazed or wounded by R.A.F. bombing, combined to make forest operations a testing experience.

The Army's operation against the Greek nationalist uprising in Cyprus was to last from 1955 to 1959, though after the ending of the Forest Emergency regiments remained committed to lesser scale operations for many years to come. The Army's roles were similar to those in Kenya. In towns regiments were tasked to secure public buildings and communications against both Greek and Turkish violence. In the two mountain forest areas, the Troodos and the Paphos, operations were section based, either in patrols or ambushes, or in large-scale cordons and sweeps in which sections formed part of a chain. In winter the two areas could be very cold, with snow on the Troodos range, in summer very hot. Operations could last many days, sometimes up to twelve weeks. Sections existed on compo either carried with them or consumed at field kitchens of various types. In one very long operation the compo was of poor quality in taste, choice and health preservation. On one occasion soldiers of one Light Infantry company developed serious boils. The Director of Medical Services directed that fresh rations providing vitamins be supplied but his efforts only resulted in sacks full of onions. Helicopter supply became available late in the campaign. In the urban areas unit and sub-unit cookhouses could draw on local meat, fruit and vegetables to supplement compo.

The last British Army colonial counter-insurgency operation was in Southern Arabia, Aden and its hinterland. From the inter-war years the hinterland area had seen local unrest and revolt, operations assuming a larger scale in 1964 and finishing abruptly in 1967. The fighting in 1964 took place in a black volcanic mountainous area sixty miles north of Aden, The Radfan, jagged hill and mountain ridges and peaks mostly ranging from 3,000 and 4,000 feet high, the highest at 5,500 feet, ideal for insurgent snipers and ambushes, interspersed with wadis and flat zones. Three British units and locally recruited levies were involved, their opponent being roving Soviet-armed nationalist bands backed by Egypt and Yemen, some equipped with more modern infantry level weapons than the British. Although the wadis provided terrain suitable for four small bases each with an airstrip, patrols and picquets sent out from the bases had on occasions to descend from hillsides by rope. Supply for forward sub-units would be on the basis of one fully fighting sub-unit operating with another of 'fighting porters' carrying food, water and ammunition on manpack frames. Water was limited to two gallons per man per day for all purposes, carried by the men themselves or flown in by light aircraft or helicopter. Food was also a complication - no one-man 24 hour packs being available, the ten-man compo packs proved very inconvenient in Radfan conditions, where the heat during the day could be so intense that an egg could be fried on the bonnet of a vehicle. Sometimes soldiers, programmed for patrolling, would assemble at the site of an air drop and, there and then, cook and eat the contents of the heavy ten-man packs in the knowledge that this was all the food that they were likely to have for the next twenty-four hours. At other times cooked food could be provided for the bases, men on patrols and ambushes on emergency small packs. The campaign was a success, the mountain area having been stabilised, and ended in October 1964 when the regiments were withdrawn to Aden.

Urban insurgency in Aden became worsened by the rivalry between two insurgent groups, both attacking the British military presence, killing a large number of servicemen and British civilians. Operations can be summed up by saying that from 1964 to 1966 regiments were concerned with clearing and dominating important areas; after the London 1966 announcement of withdrawal the concern was more with control, direct or indirect, of areas that were going to be essential for the final withdrawal of solders, some by air with the last by helicopters to Royal Navy warships.

Over ten regiments, battalions or Royal Marine Commandos together with a number of other detachments, were involved in this last 1976-67 stage of British rule in Aden. In general men were fed under unit or sub-unit arrangements. These varied very greatly but all had great difficulties in common. One camp had 1,500 men to feed, with its own ration store and butchery; it operated round the clock to suit the different operational needs of different units. Other areas fed men from field kitchens, one including trials of a new 150-man cooker. The field kitchens were set up in guarded strong points, or in one of the two cookhouses improvised in an existing shack or building. Aden's stifling heat made locally grown or purchased food including fresh vegetables short-lived and the temperatures added considerable stress to the work of cooks. Riots, strikes, snipers, ambushes for all, and, in addition for the cookhouses in buildings, water and power cuts, were the daily round.

Conventional War 1945-67

The British Army fought in three conventional wars in the years 1945 to 1968. The first of these, the most important and the bloodiest, was the Korean War.

On 25 June 1950 troops of the Communist government of North Korea invaded American-protected South Korea, intending to unify the Korean Peninsula under Communism. Two days later the United Nations authorised an international force to assist South Korea. This force, American-led and with a majority of soldiers American, included a big component of British and Commonwealth regiments. Within this component, at one time or another until the end of the fighting, served three armoured and six artillery regiments and sixteen infantry battalions of the British Army, together with Engineers, Signals and Medical units, several suffering heavy casualties.

The war fell into four different phases. At the outset the weak American and South Korean forces were pushed back into a small area on the southern coast. Then after a brilliant landing by the Americans behind the North Korean lines on the peninsula's west coast and the arrival of substantial international reinforcements, the United Nations force was able to reoccupy the South's capital Seoul, sweep the North Koreans out of South Korea and enter the North, occupying its capital Pyongyang and reaching the Korean-Chinese border. The Chinese government reacted to this by committing the Chinese Army in support of the North and in a series of attacks from late October 1950 to January 1951 pushed the United Nations force back into South Korea, again capturing Seoul, but in March the city was once more liberated and United Nations forces returned to the North South border. A final massive Chinese attack in April led to the epic last stand of the Gloucestershire Regiment and withdrawals but the United Nations forces counter-attacked in May retuning to the border. Fighting then, with the exception of two major Chinese attacks on east coast South Korean formations, became static and much reduced in scale. After fifteen months of negotiation a ceasefire in July 1953 ended the war.

The Regimental Sergeant Major of an artillery regiment turning his hand at cooking. He was apparently irritated at delays! Korea, 1951. (Brigadier B.A. Parritt)

The terrain of the Korean peninsula was difficult, with ranges of plum pudding-shaped hills some 1,000 feet high, swamps and poor roads. Perhaps even more difficult were the extremes of climate, very hot in summer but glacially cold in winter, thirty degrees of frost and an unnerving icy west wind. Egg yolks froze before cooking, a mug of tea put down for a few seconds turned to ice, tins of meat had to be soaked in boiling water for at least two hours to become even lukewarm. The first winter of the war, 1950-51, was particularly cold and testing, the chaos of the initial retreat disrupting the supply of food to regiments.

Difficulties of supply were great, the U.S. army jeeps and lorries not always equal to the poor roads. In some cases British units were supplied by air drop, in others by a tracked load carrier, the 'Oxford'. Supply routes, especially in the early months, were attacked by guerrillas. Further forward, South Korean porter labour was used, and very greatly respected for its work.

The tactical conditions imposed by the terrain also added much to the problems of food supply to the immediate front line trenches and dugouts. These were frequently bombarded, rifle platoons and companies might have to be deployed 4,000 yards forward of regimental headquarters on the slopes of a large steep hillside or in a paddy field swamp. Conditions often resembled that of the 1914-18 Western Front.

An additional problem was one of morale, not so much general complaining but more about the monotony or short supply of the food. For the war the Army had recalled a number of reservists retained on regimental lists after 1945. These were men who had established themselves in civilian and family life, some in their early or even mid-thirties who resented the disruption of recall to the Colours. A minority had records not entirely unblemished in their military or civilian past, most on recall were unfit in exacting military terms and far from enthusiastic over a return to army field rations. Resentment was expressed in grumbling, on a few occasions by the far more serious condition of no grumbling, and also on occasions in the matter of food condition or distribution by individual 'me first' incidents, and on one occasion by a serious soldiers' protest over corned beef that was inedible. Gestures and protests ended when the unit was in battle. In theory two ration scales, for summer and for cold weather, were eventually set out, coming into effect only after the heavy fighting was over (a special ration scale of meat, biscuits and green vegetables was also set out for 'War Dogs'). Water was not usually a major problem, though it had to be purified if taken from local rivers and soldiers were issued with water purifying kits for emergency use.

The food supplied to the British battalions varied very greatly according to the ebb and flow of the war and supplies. The first three British battalions to arrive, the Argyll and Sutherland Highlanders, the Middlesex Regiment and the Royal Ulster Rifles, forming 27th Brigade, all lived on American Combat Upgrade (CU) 24 hour combat packs throughout the severe winter of 1950. These packs, including a very valuable tin opener, contained packages of chicken noodles or tinned pork chops, beans, spaghetti, fruit or fruit juice, sugar, cigarettes and coffee. This was not always popular with the soldiers, the food except the fruit, being too highly spiced and there was neither tea nor powdered milk. The Highlanders, in particular, and many others, more accustomed to cereals or porridge, had pork slices, grapefruit

A party given by an artillery regiment for Korean children – note the dixies and Carnation milk. (Brigadier B.A. Parritt)

and tinned tomatoes for breakfast and later for the evening main meal tins of hashed meat of various types, chicken, hamburger meat, veal and spaghetti, or most commonly turkey, also unpopular with Scottish soldiers. Quantities of fruit juice, cigarettes and coffee were always included but to the British soldier this was never the same as a 'brew up' of tea. The only fresh fruit occasionally available were Korean apples; injudicious use of these 'requisitioned' apples led to dysentery outbreaks among consumers. At the same time, in another sector held by 29 Brigade, the Gloucestershire Regiment were defending an area they later came to call 'Compo Valley' living on nothing but British bully beef, soya sausage, tinned steak and kidney pudding and biscuits supplemented by dehydrated potatoes and sometimes poor quality bacon. The compo rations, when they arrived, came in five varieties but were generally felt to be leftover from the war, including powdered potato, dried egg, tinned meat and tubes of an evil-tasting condensed milk. Imagination was needed to make palatable meals, fritters and stews from such tins as arrived. At first these rations were sent to outlying platoons in hay boxes carried by South Korean porters, then Company cooking points were set up, some using the very efficient American Army M 1937 'Tent Stove' which could be fuelled on petrol, diesel or with the fuel burner's detached wood. In time food again improved with supplementary American rations and on occasions local sausages, chicken and meat and vegetables. Tea, condensed milk and sugar were now always to hand. A Korean version of the oil drum 'Benghazi burner' also came into use. A daily rum issue was provided and in quiet periods soldiers experimented with a local firewater, 'Korean Scotch', a drink so dangerous that it was officially forbidden. In its defensive position at the start of the Imjin Battle the Glosters were distributed in platoon positions; the sentries' foxholes some four to five foot deep having within them a hole scooped out in which a small wood fire could be lit burning straw, the smoke escaping through a small vent in the roof. When the mass Chinese attacks began most of the Regiment's soldiers were without sleep or food for two days, a fortunate few being provided with water and hard boiled eggs or the remains of American ration fruit or chocolate. Air supply could not be effected in view of the artillery barrages. Some 500 men of the battalion, including a number wounded, passed into Chinese captivity, all very hungry and thirsty.

In the trench war period NAAFI canteens were permitted to come a little distance behind the lines; not bound by regulations. 'Sally Anns', Salvation Army vehicles, dispensed 'char and wads' to forward units every ten days or so.

Some accounts, particularly those written by soldiers and war correspondents rather than officers, seem to indicate that the Korean War contributed to a change in officer-soldier relationships. These accounts note resentment when in quiet periods officers retreated to improvised officers' messes with slightly greater warmth, better food or spirit drinks. It would seem that not all officers had absorbed the lesson of the 1945 General Election, though of course all officers shared all the misfortunes of their men in the heat of battle. Certainly accounts of campaigns after 1950 do not mention this issue again; one may speculate that a lesson was drawn from the War.

The first military attack on Egypt in early November 1956 followed the decision of the Egyptian government headed by Colonel Nasser to nationalise the Suez Canal, at that time an international waterway. The three nations involved in the conflict, Great Britain, France and Israel, had different agendas; that of Britain was stated to be the prevention, by physical intervention, of an Arab-Israel conflict that might close the Canal. Covertly London shared the aspiration, more openly expressed by the French and Israelis, that the assault would lead to the fall of Colonel Nasser. The assault on 5 November led to sharp but brief fighting and a ceasefire following intense United Nations and United States pressure. An Arab Israel conflict had been prevented for ten years but Colonel Nasser remained in power.

The operation itself involved the descent by British and French elite *Coloniale* and Foreign Legion parachute troops with also the landing, part by assault over a beach and part by helicopter, of the Royal Marines and more parachuted French troops in three areas around Port Said. The descents and landings were followed by the occupation of Port Said itself and an advance down the Canal was begun. Further regiments of both armies then began to arrive, transported by sea, but after a day's fighting the ceasefire was imposed. The build-up of British troops continued for several days with some street clashes continuing until withdrawal on the 22 December.

Soldiers in the assaults carried, in addition to their own and section weapons, a shovel, two full water bottles and two 24 hour ration packs. As the town became stabilised regiments were able to cook or at least brew up tea and warm up compo rations. Supply was relatively straightforward, initially helicopters from the armada of warships, later by direct unloading. A section of the Guards Parachute Company operating with the French were able to enjoy French rations including wine, as essential to the French soldiers as tea for the British.

The last of the British Army's Far East Campaigns was a conventional war although fought in jungle conditions. In the colonial era the northern parts of the island of Borneo had been under British rule or protection, the larger southern parts of the island were, following the end of Netherland colonial rule, part of the new state of Indonesia. The Indonesians laid claim to the whole island, first by infiltration into the Bornean British areas and then by the use of professional soldiers of the Indonesian Army. The terrain over which the campaign was fought was mostly mountainous jungle with a few areas of rubber plantations and rice paddy fields, punctuated by rivers and swamps. The jungle was dense, dangerous and disease ridden, very hot by day but cold at night with frequent heavy rainfall. Animal life varied from orang-utans and pythons to mosquitoes and leeches. Much of the local water was dangerous, as in Malaya in many areas it was life-threatening to drink. A soldier caught drinking local water was often put on a charge.

The pattern of operations was one of fortified Forward Locality Bases, perimeters sandbagged, within which were machine guns, mortars, field artillery and in some areas medium guns, base and regimental headquarters and first-aid posts together with a helicopter landing zone nearby. From these bases patrols of varying sizes would be sent out, initially for three days but with growing expertise up to ten or twelve days, if near an enemy unit even longer. Ambushes would be laid, the distance in the jungle between Indonesian intruders and British soldiers being sometimes only a few feet. Supply was by aircraft or helicopter, either in a forest clearing or lowered from the machine.

The bases provided a field cookhouse, a stove and ovens in a long dugout in the ground with a layout of a Calor gas pipe fuelling a set of burners cooking food in twenty gallon dixies. Food was good but tended to be monotonous. European theatre compo 24 hour ten-man patrol packs provided cereals and a cooked breakfast, a snack lunch and a two course evening meal of hot meat and a dried vegetable dish followed by a pudding. A bakery was opened locally. In some bases an adjoining canteen provided local 'Tiger' beer, though a limit of two cans at any one time was generally imposed; in other bases alcohol was banned. In 1965 the lightweight jungle ration pack using local resources that had been introduced in the last years of the Malaysian campaign were issued to some regiments and bases containing fresh meat, eggs and vegetables. These proved more popular than the compo dehydrated vegetables, being more easily digestible in the heat. When its smell did not give away positions and in the bases, curry powder was added to evening meals.

Out on patrols smoking or brewing a tin of tea on a hexamine burner was again only allowed if the patrol commander so permitted, main meal ration packs, again if permitted at all, were eaten cold. Curry powder was not allowed and even the smell of an opened tin of meat could be a give-away. Army cheese proved popular and useful in these conditions, dried octopus was however not appreciated. Frequently after a cold meat dinner soldiers had to lie out in the cold and rain with only a ground sheet for protection.

On some occasions patrol ration packs had to be left concealed in the undergrowth so that the patrol could move more quickly without give-away baggage to an ambush position, or patrols simply left bases with only half rations. Soldiers would then be reduced to biscuits and chocolate carried in their pockets and water in their bottles for several days until an air drop could be authorised. Only very limited distance cross-border entry into Indonesian Borneo was allowed for ambush or in hot pursuit and nothing that could identify the British troops could be left behind; used ration packs had to be taken back across the border. After patrolling on less than 2,000 calories per day soldiers needed a recuperative period on good food in one of the Forward Locality Bases before further operations. The medical officer of the 2nd Parachute Regiment assessed that a soldier could exist on 900 calories a day for ten days, losing a pound a day in weight, but replacing it all quickly on return to base.

Political changes in Indonesia brought about an end to the conflict.

8

The Post-War Years: 1968–2010

After one year of peace, 1968, that followed the end of the Borneo War, the Army was to find itself heavily committed in six conflicts, each very different from any of the others, a long counter-terrorist campaign in Northern Ireland, limited conventional wars in the Falkland Islands and Iraq, military peace-keeping in the former Yugoslavia, a regime change and its consequences in Iraq and a conflict against Muslim fundamentalists in Afghanistan, at the time of writing ongoing.

Northern Ireland

The regiments deployed tour after tour in containing the extreme sectarian violence in the province of Northern Ireland were involved in three types of operations, ones set in the rain-swept streets of Belfast and Londonderry, others in the countryside and towns of rural Northern Ireland, and again others along the border with the Republic of Ireland, known to soldiers as 'Bandit Country'. An unusual difficulty arose when a very large-scale operation, such as the 1972 *Motorman* clearing roadblocks and ending 'no go' areas in Londonderry was being planned. Such absolute secrecy over the preparations had to be observed that local supply staff officers could only be told at the very last minute of the number of soldiers who would require feeding. Guessing was usually but not always right.

In the cities and towns units and sub-units established themselves in old buildings, often empty and dirty mills, factories, disused schools and later in fortified 'sangar' bases. A big Royal Navy former submarine depot ship, H.M.S. *Maidstone*, was also used. From these bases patrols would be sent out with 24 hour packs and water bottles for a tea brew-up on hexamine stoves. Patrols would man road checkpoints, control invective shouting, missile throwing and dustbin lid clanging, street riots, search premises for terrorists or weapons, guard detention centres, demolish barricades and pursue petrol bombers. On the border, sometimes under mortar or machine-gun fire from within the Republic, soldiers manned border checkpoints and high-rise watch towers, and mounted patrols and ambushes against weapon smugglers. Sometimes a company Colour Sergeant would follow out to provide them with fresh food. In the bases new cookers, the No 4 which could cater for one hundred and fifty men and the No 5 catering for thirty-five, could be used aboard *Maidstone*, where there were of course fully operational 'galleys' for cooking. On land the No 4 cooker using Calor gas was often mounted on a trailer when units had to be on the move. Elsewhere large portakabins came into use in bases, the first to arrive in 1972 immediately had all its windows smashed by stone-throwing children. Catering Corps cooks attached to infantry battalions shared the same hazards, facing missiles and incendiary bombs. One field kitchen was blown-up by a car bomb and on several occasions cooks had to turn to the defence of their bases. Later, for patrols tasked for shorter periods, soldiers could set out with packed food meals, returning to bases for hot food. Fresh eggs and bread were always available to make the ever-popular 'banjos', egg sandwiches. By the mid-1970s robust ten litre food containers, the cavity between the inner and outer parts filled with foam, came into service. By the 1980s unbreakable vacuum flasks were available, soldiers then being able to carry hot drinks in their day packs. Soldiers were allowed two cans of beer every 24 hours, the 'two cans a day' soon becoming a standard for most, but not all later operations.

The Falkland Islands

In April 1982 Argentinian troops invaded the British-owned South Atlantic Falkland Islands, proclaiming their annexation. A resolute British government decided upon liberation and a Royal Navy transported task force was despatched, the ground force contingent initially based upon three Royal Marine Commandos and two Parachute Regiment battalions together with sub-units, to be joined later by two Guards battalions and one of Gurkha infantry. The long distance, stormy seas and cold weather were all difficulties for the force.

The landings on the islands were shelled but not directly opposed by Argentinian ground troops but they were continuously attacked from the air. Regiments and individuals experienced differing fortunes. Some had travelled to the theatre in requisitioned liners or other ships in comfort, others less so in warships. Some were able to descend from ships by rope into landing craft with short boat journeys and little inconvenience. The Scots Guards, however, spent seven hours travelling in open landing craft in heavy seas and heavy rain with no food, hot or cold. Regiments landed with a 48 hour Arctic ration pack of soup and a roll together with a hexamine burner to provide three snacks a day. Then followed half Arctic rations and after the sixth day full Arctic rations. Compo ration main meal dishes now appeared in convenient packs that could be boiled in the pack, the hot water then being to hand for tea.

Soldier of the 3rd Battalion the Parachute Regiment eating dinner in the Woolshed, Port San Carlos, Falklands War. (Lt Gen Sir Hew Pike)

The battalions ashore, operations took on an almost old-fashioned style of infantry war, two uniformed armies over peat-bog ground, rough but very sparsely populated, with two or more battalion-sized pitched battles at Goose Green and at Mount Tumbledown and Longdon, very long approach marches, and one seriously damaging Argentinian air attack at Bluff Cove. The weather was very cold, units often had to remain in wet clothes in even wetter trenches for long periods between marches.

The high calorie value Arctic rations were dehydrated and light to carry, essential in an operation involving so much long distance marching. They were however later to be the cause of unexpected stomach trouble when soldiers returned to fresh food. The speed at which the campaign had to be conducted, allowing only few and very brief rest periods, was a further factor. The daily ration in 24 hour packs varied but essentially provided a hot breakfast of rolled oats with milk and sugar, lemon essence together with drinking chocolate, biscuits and a cheese or meat spread snack lunch, and a hot evening meal of soup, one of four varieties of meat granules—some curried, dehydrated vegetables, rice or potatoes, apple flakes (which some added to the morning oatmeal), coffee, tea, Bovril, a confectionary bar, nuts and raisins. In the long marches - 'tabbing' to the Army, 'yomping' to the Marines – conducted mostly in darkness, snacks would be eaten on the march. Soldiers set out carrying two days' rations but re-supply was not always able to catch up for a day or more; the soldiers of the 2nd Parachute Regiment attacking at Goose Green were not able to have a full meal before the attack. Cooks became stretcher-bearers, four being killed. Apart from an unlucky sheep or goose and occasional onions and potatoes local additions were rare. Some units were able to set up field kitchens for one or two companies in tents with No 1 burners but fuel was not always to hand. Others improvised cookers were made from hand grenade tins or other containers. The Scots Guards engaged in the major formal attack on Mount Tumbledown had a centralised full meat meal before the operation began. The 3rd Parachute Regiment's companies were more widely scattered, and the pre-attack meal was prepared on local sites. Large quantities of hot tea were rushed forward to the survivors from the support ship *Sir Galahad* after it was set on fire by Argentinian aircraft. Captured Argentinian officers' food, notably huge cheeses and brandy, were available at the end of the campaign, but the Argentinian wine was rated barely drinkable.

Water was frequently a problem however, becoming stuck in mud and bogs. The local water was brackish and produced a condition known politely as 'Galtieri's Revenge', the purifying tablets having only limited effect. Although it should not have done the conflict came as a surprise to London. Ships were packed in haste, not necessarily in a proper order, causing great confusion upon arrival. The important storeship carrying helicopters was sunk by Argentinian aircraft. Once the landings were firmly established, a supply chain became organised. Food was landed from supply ships in small landing craft, or large 125 foot long powered rafts known as Mexeflotes and capable of carrying 150 tons of supplies, or, if available, by helicopters. Argentinian daytime airpower necessitated supply ships unloading at night. Supplies were then taken from the beaches to dumps on tracked Volvo BU202 vehicles, occasionally needing the help of local farm tractors, and thereafter on to regiments. As noted earlier, food available to groups and individuals could vary according to operations and duties - one Intelligence Corps warrant officer triumphantly entered Port Stanley with just a Mars Bar in his pocket. Although victorious it was a weary, cold and hungry army that ended the mercifully short campaign.

Iraq 1991

The first Iraq War, 1990-91 was caused by the Iraqi invasion of Kuwait and a subsequent United Nations authorisation of a military force to eject the invaders and restore Kuwait's independence. The British Army's main frontline contribution was two armoured brigades and a large artillery group together with intelligence and special forces personnel; the bulk of the mult-national force was American and was led by an American general. The last month of the 1990 war was a period of build-up of forces, the short-lived military campaign took place in February 1991 when by day heat was fierce and at night the rain and cold penetrating.

A soldier of the Royal Scots Dragoon Guards has an American MRE meal during the Gulf War, February 1991. (Major Aidan Stephen)

The long Cold War in Germany with its emphasis on the possibility of armoured warfare had led to a massive improvement in food supply; tanks and armoured personnel carriers carried food and water and were equipped with on-board cookers for a quick brew of tea or, if conditions permitted, heating a cold compo ration. On a daily rota basis one member of a tank's crew would be the cook. The British Army's compo rations were greatly superior to the lightweight American Meals Ready to Eat (MRE) which were easy to cook but often eaten cold, and lacked bulk, leaving the soldiers feeling half-starved. Americans referred to their MRE as 'Meals Rejected by Ethiopians'. Americans were glad to obtain compo whenever they could while British soldiers valued MRE as useful for a snack. The Americans, wearied by turkey, regarded corned beef as a welcome change. In the later build-up period the British ten-man compo ration boxes arrived and were supplemented by fresh food and cooked at unit or sub-unit level on lorry-borne mobile cookers three times a day by the sub-unit Quartermaster Sergeant, the issue being carefully controlled and soldiers being provided with disposable plates, knives and forks. In armoured vehicles food might be heated up within the vehicle itself. When battle was joined, the fresh food had to be much reduced and soldiers remained on compo, arriving in boxes of various sizes and edible cold or hot. Brigadier Cordingley and others record the typical day's rations as a breakfast of tinned sausage or a processed bacon grill with beans, lunch a cheese or jam sandwich and an evening meal, heated if circumstances permitted, of beef either with spices, or onions or kidneys in a suet pudding, beefburgers, pork chops, chicken prepared in a few different ways, tinned fruit or a solid pudding. The all-important tea, supplied in large bags, came with each meal. The limited variety did not however overcome a certain weariness with these prepared meals and many soldiers were unenthusiastic. The experience here confirmed the view that had been forming since the introduction of compo. Compo (and MRE) were liked but eaten less in combat or active service, while in rest or in a base they were less liked but more was actually eaten—a reflection of the circumstances of food consumption. Soldiers were well provided with good quality water, at least two litres per day.

In the build-up period the Army hired a very large cold store which enabled the supply staff to buy, after checking against any poisoning, and keep fresh eggs, fruit and vegetables for onward despatch to forward units in base camps. A force bakery supplied fresh bread and rolls. Food supplies, together with other stores and ammunition, were flown in by an international armada of aircraft and then moved forward to regiments.

The most serious problem, as in 1916 and 1920, was water. The Royal Engineers had to develop wells, negotiating with their owners, and much time and energy then had to be devoted to fitting out conversion plants, in technical terms 'reverse osmosis' to convert brackish water into drinkable clean water. Supply transport proved to be a difficulty, British lorries designed for West Germany sank into the sand or after heavy rain swamp ground and American tracked vehicles had to borrowed.

The campaign drew on great popular support in Britain both from institutions such as the Royal British Legion and newspapers and ordinary members of the public who sent parcels, particularly over the 1991 Christmas period. The campaign, mounted from a strictly Muslim country, had been declared to be 'dry', with no rum issue or availability of beer (other than non-alcoholic). Cakes and Christmas pudding were however often well-laced and not subject to regulations.

Bosnia-Herzegovina

British Army regiments served in the United Nations and NATO groupings at work in the 'muscular peacekeeping' operation that followed the break-up of the former Yugoslavia. The work involved protection of communities under threat from the rival local armies, Croat, Bosnian, Muslim and Serb, interpositioning, keeping roads free from mines and checkpoints, and trying to distinguish between Muslim and Serb corpses for proper burials. Peace enforcement in 'someone else's' war was often dangerous, the Army losing a small number killed. In winter extreme cold and deep snow made the soldier's life, particularly those on patrol or observation points, very hard, water freezing rock-solid in jerry cans, making even a brew-up often difficult, at times impossible.

Regiments generally centred on deserted schools, factories or administrative office premises. Some units received the new HESCO field shelters, developed from the road construction industry. These were erected around lightweight steel cage boxes with sides made from bags filled with rubble or stones, offering some protection as well as shelter, particularly if they were dug in. Other units less fortunate had to spend weeks in tents. Compo rations could sometimes be supplemented with local seasonal products, eggs, fruit and vegetables to provide the necessary vitamins. But, certainly at the outset, the meat content of the ten-man packs appears to have been poor, greasy and full of fat, soldiers whenever possible preferring the snack of a sausage and egg 'banjo' sandwich and a mug of tea kept hot in their vacuum mugs. Later food conditions in bases improved, and soldiers very appreciative of the work of their cooks.

Mules can replenish those places to which motor vehicles cannot travel. Gorazde, Bosnia, 1995.
(Royal Welch Fusiliers)

One regiment's experience of Bosnia was however, although small-scale, epic, the 1st Royal Welch Fusiliers having to endure, with the exception of the Welsh Guards in the Falklands, at the time the toughest experience of any British battalion since the end of the Korean War. The battalion was tasked to secure the Muslim population of the Bosnian town of Gorazde. Before the collapse of the Yugoslav state the town had been in a Muslim area but its inhabitants included a large Serb population. In the earlier months of conflict a Muslim army had brought about the almost total expulsion or flight of the Serb population; the Muslims aspired to link up with another Muslim region to the south with a view to further expansion. A strong and capably-led Serb army sought to retake the town and laid siege to it. Under NATO orders the Royal Welch Fusiliers were directed to observe and monitor a safe area agreement, arriving to relieve another battalion on 1 March 1995. The local terrain was one of steep hills, the highest almost 3,000 feet. The first three months saw routine peacekeeping with a number of detached observation posts but also occasional shooting incidents with the Serbs. At the end of May the Serb General Mladic launched a general attack. taking fusiliers hostage, obliging some immediate and later the complete withdrawal of the observation posts. Continuous Serbian artillery fire in and around the battalion area necessitated much of the battalion living under cover in First World War-style protected dugouts for thirty days until late July, when very firm diplomatic processes were applied to Mladic. Conditions, though, still remained difficult and dangerous until the withdrawal of the battalion following further international negotiations at the end of August.

In April food was prepared in a tented kitchen or portable cookers fuelled either by gas of petrol, together with a six foot long concrete fireplace, improved a little later by a prefabricated cooking unit, but the fireplace had to remain in continuous use. As the Serb blockade tightened fuel for the cookers became short and cooking turned to wood supply, both for the fireplace and oil drums used as 'Benghazi Burners'. For soldiers in the headquarters area two main and one snack meal per day were prepared, for soldiers when in the scattered observation posts food, soup and tea had to be despatched out in various containers. Fuel restrictions came increasingly to preclude the use of the battalion's vehicles, experiments with carts was not a success. Mules were used to supply some posts, for others the containers had to be carried out to the posts by soldiers over the very difficult ground.

Even before the main Serb attack food and fuel supply for the battalion had been difficult. The last fresh food supply arrived on 24 April after a three-week blockade, and a convoy that arrived on 2 May included food amounting to only twenty-five percent of the weekly rations needed by the battalion. On 14 May the commanding officer reduced daily rations by one-third, a reduction worsened by the ending of any supply of fresh fruit or vegetables. A mash made from potato powder and local water, named 'Drina Mash' after the local river, was said by soldiers to have a second use in the construction of bomb-proof dugouts. The Regiment's cooks did their best with what they had and well deserved the battalion's commanding officer's tribute that they were the "unsung heroes" of Gorazde.

The strains, of food lacking vitamins, cold storage and the water purifier shut down from shortage of fuel, bombardments and a dugout life, and the altitude, for which soldiers should have had more water than was available, were all extremely testing. Despite the arrival on 25 June of a French Army relief column—with the encouraging message " Allo Wellington, ici Napoleon"—bringing a few days' worth of food, mostly pasta and sufficient fuel for a month, conditions remained very severe. Bosnian Muslims now turned on to those that had been protecting them. The damage that had been done was, however, evident from the outcome - the number of soldiers affected by the appearance of the serious vitamin deficiency disease, scurvy. Many, including the commanding officer, lost hair and teeth.

Army public relations accounts of this extraordinary contemporary medical occurrence remained economic with the truth.

Iraq 2003-2007

The British Army joined the American-led 'Coalition' force invading Iraq in 2003, argument at the time claiming the regime of the monstrously despotic Iraqi leader, Saddam Hussein, possessed weapons of mass destruction. Victory over Saddam was achieved quickly but his fall, that of the regime and the disbanding of the Iraqi Army left a deep political vacuum in which factions soon emerged to fight for power in different areas and if coalition forces were trying to maintain an impartial order in an area, to fight against them also.

The British were allotted the Basra area and the Maysan province in the north, both with a large majority Shia Muslim population and both provinces adjoining the Iran border. The provinces, eighty percent Shia, were divided by local ethnicity, family and religious interests and jealousies but all were determined never to return to the seventy-five years of Sunni rule that had followed the post-First World War creation of the state of Iraq. After a brief 'honeymoon' period following their liberation from the Sunni, Shia militias, in particular the Mahdi Army, began to turn on the British regiments; they were equipped with modern Soviet weapons left from Saddam's army, and with further weapons smuggled in from Iran. Attacks on the British began in April 2004 and became very much more serious in August with ambushes, grenade and mortar attacks, and later to include roadside bombs and suicide bombings of various types. For the British regiments it was war amidst the people, a square here calm, the next square sullen and a third a fiery ambush or a very hostile crowd. Street battles, although small-scale, were vicious, involving armoured vehicles, tanks and on occasions strike aircraft and resulting in a number of casualties, killed, severely wounded or burnt. After much determined fighting the British Army, outnumbered and badly resourced, was forced to leave Maysan in August 2006 and then operate in Basra under American command before final withdrawal.

The early entry into Basra was straightforward. An account published later by the First Fusiliers Battle Group records that soldiers in the initial operation were living on 24 hour ration packs in a camp where fresh food was available for breakfast and supper, with American MRE's, a system which provides a meal drawing no distinction between breakfast, lunch or supper, available for snacks. This MRE 'one meal fits all' offered twenty-six varieties of food, together with a flameless cooker and a spoon. Iced tea, impossible to brew-up, and peanut butter were not, however, to everyone's taste and the British were relieved when Army 'Slops jockeys' took over from the Americans to work in a huge cooking tent preparing a hot breakfast and evening meal for over 10,000 men.

Further north in Maysan provincial capital, Al Amrah, a battle group built around the 1st Princess of Wales' Royal Regiment established accommodation itself in a vast former Iraq military camp, with one detachment in the centre of town for liaison with the local authorities and another guarding the nearby airstrip. Within the main camp air-conditioned HESCO blocks and tents provided shelter and some measure of cover with sangars manned day and night for perimeter defence. In the accommodation for security reasons only one quarter of the soldiers could eat at any one time, the food being taken out to those on guard duty in large green insulated boxes and eaten under cover. Soldiers commented on the excellent quality of fish and chips, beefburgers, pizzas, spaghetti Bolognese, three hot meals a day with numerous choices, cheese cake and ice cream, although in the hot weather flies and the heat in the cookhouse were highly unpleasant. At times compo rations were sufficiently warm not to require heating, and water in water bottles ready for a tea 'brew-up'. The camp was well supplied with bottled water. Some soldiers received a bottle of whisky from friends or relations in Britain. Local Iraqi entrepreneurs also offered whisky of dubious quality—and also Viagara tablets. Occasionally American M.R.E.'s were available, some by barter, others having 'fallen off the back of a lorry'.

The detachment in the centre of the town in a strongly fortified house were before long reduced to ration packs with one meal of fresh food per day prepared on a mobile kitchen trailer. The ingredients of this meal, together with cold drinks and chocolate, were brought to the detachment at night in armoured Landrovers or Warrior tracked armoured fighting vehicles. Both the camp and the town detachment were permanently the target of mortar and artillery bombardment, the detachment's cookhouse receiving a direct hit on one occasion, reducing menus to boil in the bag stews with Tabasco sauce warmed up on an improvised burner.

The number of British troops that could be made available was inadequate for the increasing number of contesting militia and forces in Maysan province and in Basra, and British forces signed off control of the area in December 2007.

Afghanistan 2006 to 2011, the time of writing

On 9th September 2001 the United States was attacked by aircraft hijacked by members of Al Qaeda, Muslim fundamentalist fanatics, the aircraft crashing into the World Trade Organization twin towers in New York and into the Pentagon. The United Stated having ascertained that the hijacking pilots had been trained in Afghanistan invoked the mutual defence clause of the NATO Treaty and sought support for military action from member nations in Afghanistan in 2003. British armed forces accordingly became committed. Afghanistan was at the time governed by the Taliban, a local extreme fundamentalist group that had accommodated Al Qaeda training camps. It was thought, at the time, that the liberation of the country would be swift, no one envisaged the protracted and bloody war against the Taliban that followed.

A single British battalion was sent to Kabul in 2003. In April 2006, although still heavily engaged in Iraq, a 3,700 strong brigade force was sent to the southern province of Helmand, an area half the size of England and one of dry, hot and dusty flat land intersected by rivers, canals and navigation ditches ideal for concealment. The population included Taliban, warring civilians and drug dealers with an economy based on opium poppies. The brigade was to enter and to remain in this second war with crippling constraints upon the numbers and equipment needed. Afghan Army units sent for training and support varied very greatly in quality. The first battle group based around the 3rd Parachute Regiment arrived in the base area Camp Bastion, at the time only poor quality tents, with for two weeks a diet limited to ration packs. As more units arrived these were deployed to Forward Operation Bases and platoon houses constructed of HESCO, with protection later rebranded as patrol bases. The aspiration had been that companies and platoons would be able to spread out and dominate areas patrolling, searching for weapons and arresting insurgents, so enabling economic and social development to take place. There were some notable successes, some only temporary. Detachments of ten to twenty men would be sent to these patrol bases with emergency ration food and water for up to two weeks. In many area, however, this aim could not be achieved or held with the manpower and helicopters available while Taliban attacks increased in skill and ferocity with heavy mortar bombardments, snipers and grenade throwers, ambushes and sophisticated roadside bomb devices. Vehicle supply to bases and platoon houses became so hazardous that helicopter fire support and supply was continuously needed, casualty figures rose, platoon houses and bases intended to be sally ports from which sections could operate became perforce heavily protected defensive positions often needing a relief operation, and the movement of supply and relief personnel became severely strained. One company tasked for a three-day task at one base found itself in the base for six weeks. Areas initially occupied had to be abandoned, soldiers became increasingly exhausted, casualty figures rose.

An officer of 13 Company, 15 (Airborne) Signals Regiment, cooking a meal, Kajaki Dam operation, Afghanistan 2008. (Royal Logistics Corps)

Initially the soldiers in the forward bases and the platoon houses supplied for them were provided with adequate compo rations but food and water soon became short, water just one bottle a day, two, sometimes only one, boil in the bag hot meals per day, corned beef hash, hotpot, chicken pasta, bacon and beans, water biscuits and pate, and chocolate if it had not already melted in the heat. The food was monotonous and lacking in vitamins, it was sharply criticized by visiting inspecting officers. As time passed and the fighting intensified as the Taliban acquired a range of mortars and more skilled commanders, vehicle supply to the forward bases had to be replaced with helicopter drops, but units were still limited to one or two boil in the bag meals per day with limited fresh fruit and vegetables. Some bases received cooking equipment, others turned to traditional improvised oil drum stoves, much equipment from Britain arrived later. One regiment, the Coldstream Guards, made a point of supplying a smaller base with a change of food once a month, this involved a journey in heavily armed convoy with personnel wearing body armour. Detachments were on rotation sent back to Camp Bastion for a, usually very brief, period giving men rest, good food and personal washing. The total strength of the British brigade contingent was to rise to over 9,000 but the number remained inadequate for the area and the fighting increasingly heavy and intense. At the time of writing, July 2011, three hundred and twenty seven British servicemen have been killed and scores more severely injured and areas formerly under British military control passed to the Americans, in others local administration has been handed over to the Afghans. The smaller areas left to British battalions enabled a more effective control to be mounted in towns and villages which are planned to be taken over on the British withdrawal.

Camp Bastion has grown to be the largest and most elaborate military encampment since the Second World War housing at various peak periods up to 6,000 personnel (including civil contractors and labour). Besides temporary accommodation buildings facilities include, at the time of writing, a full field surgical hospital, a Chinook heavy lift helicopter squadron, a water treatment plant, a gymnasium and a special American food centre. A large tented dining area is divided into four, two areas serving the same choice of food, two a lighter meal. Behind the tents is a cooking area, tasked to produce four meals a day, the fourth being late night and reserved for personnel arriving or returning late. Each meal offers a variety of meat, fish, curry and vegetarian dishes with fresh vegetables. All ranks mess in common. An average 12,000 meals per day are provided for the defence company or personnel passing through. The quantities are staggering, 7,500 burgers, 20,000 baguettes and four and a half tonnes of potatoes and chips per week, ten tonnes of chicken breast per month. Almost all supplies have to be flown in, vehicle supply being too dangerous. Some personnel in the camp on immediate stand-by have to remain in their special accommodation, food being brought to them. No alcohol is available, however, a number of newly arriving personnel bring with them a bottle for emergencies or celebrations.

These Camp Bastion Base facilities should not obscure the hard, gruesome and often chaotic realities of the campaign. For the British, small in relative scale, the operations, food and life of the Forward Observation Base, patrol bases and checkpoints were as grim the Western Front trenches of the First World War. Well planned and sudden enemy attacks, the pain and agonising death or injury of friends, the vermin, dirt and stench, heat and cold, apprehension and fear, and frustration that gains made at cost had to be abandoned were all present, and in combination with concerns about the future purpose of the campaign as a whole have imposed physical fatigue and psychological stress greater than any campaign since 1945. Conditions were not helped by a careless June 2011 Ministry of Defence comment that "fat can be trimmed" from the British deployment in Afghanistan, specifically noting cooks.

An example of the compo rations issued to British soldiers serving in Afghanistan appears in an Appendix.

Conclusion

The earliest formal worldwide order instructing the British Army on field rations was issued in 1816, and signed by the Secretary for War Palmerston. The daily ration for which the taxpayer would be paying was simple, one pound of bread or biscuits, one pound of meat fresh or salted, one pint of wine and one-third of a pint of spirits. It was added with emphasis that on no account should anything else be provided. While many might regret the disappearance of the last two items, no one will disagree with the argument that food for the soldier has greatly improved over two hundred years.

In the period covered by this work, the food supply in Afghanistan completes a steady progress beginning after the Boer War. With some unfortunate exceptions the British Army has tried to ensure that food reaching the front line is adequate, even if often monotonous. But as this work has also shown poor planning and battlefield and local geographic conditions have frequently made proper supply difficult, in some cases impossible. Much effort has been made to supply armoured units far forward, and with the introduction of compo rations much greater variety became possible. Soldiers of other Allied armies—and our enemies—have been envious.

A major reason for this standard has been that the British Army is, except in major war, essentially a volunteer army; if a non-compulsory army is the only politically-acceptable army its conditions of service must be attractive. As the twentieth century, with its two World Wars, progressed social factors pushed change further. The August 1914 soldier accepted that a normal if unfortunate condition of society led to a difference between the foods which officers and soldiers could eat in the field. Very soon after 1914 the basic food for men in the trenches became in practice the same for all ranks, supplemented only by any extra an officer or soldier might receive from local or home sources. These supplements became less in the Second World War and by 2010 had almost vanished. The post-war appearance of women in forward areas and the broader social basis from which officers were recruited has also contributed to equality.

On a wider social perspective, the soldier of 1914, and to only a smaller degree less so the soldier of 1939, had often come from rough living conditions including hunger. Photographs of soldiers in the two world wars show men of generally shorter and slimmer stature than the more solid, sturdy build of soldiers serving in the late 20th and early 21st Century. The ordinary soldier's ability to survive battlefield hardship appears to be the same, but expectations are very different. The pre-1930s barrack room food system would in the early 21st Century bring voluntary recruitment to an immediate stop. The 21st Century soldier will put up with the most severe combat conditions if he sees this as necessary, but he expects at least the same food standards as the rest of British society at all other times.

Political and military leaders who neglect or overlook this expectation do so at great risk both to the nation's defence and general security, and to soldiers' lives and health.

Appendix

A ration pack as issued by British troops serving in Afghanistan 2010

The contents are packed in a waterproof cardboard box measuring 22x19x11 cm, which is labelled

24 Hour Multiclimate Ration
Menu 6

On one side of the box is a note stating that over the 38 MCR menus the mean average nutritional value equates to 4,000 Kcals, 550 gm carbohydrate, 133 gm fat and a 100 gm protein. A section 'Top Tips' urges the user to consume all the contents to gain maximum benefit, to stay well hydrated and ensure others do, and to eat as much of each retort pouch as possible as these contain high levels of carbohydrate releasing 'the energy you need to keep going'. On another side of the box the soldier is invited to complete a questionnaire for opinions on the future development of rations, the questionnaire being inside the box.

Contents with Country of Origin

Meal Pouches
    Natural Muesli 100g with skimmed milk powder (New Zealand)
    Chicken Yellow Curry Rice, 300g with rice, potato, carrot, beans oils, spices, shrimp paste, chilli (Denmark)
    Pilau Rice, 100g with onion, oils, ginger puree, garlic puree (U.K)
    Pasta Salad, 300g including semolina wheat pasta, tomatoes, basil parmesan cheese, garlic, oil, pinenuts (New Zealand)
    Pineapples in Syrup 150g (Thailand)

Snacks

>Mango, Apple, Bananas, Concentrate Fruit Puree, 90g (Denmark)
>Strawberry Fruit Bar (U.K.)
>Golden Oats Snack Bar 50g (U.K.)
>Fruit and Oat Snack Bar 50g (U.K.)
>Ginger Biscuit 50g (U.K.)
>Dark Choc Chip Biscuit (U.K.)
>Mixed Nuts 60g (U.K.)

Drinks

>Lucozade Sport Body Fuel Orange Isotonic (U.K.)
>Lemon Energy Drink (Norway) (U.K.)
>Hot Chocolate Orange 60g (Germany)
>Blackcurrant Water Flavour (U.K.)

Sundries

>4 x Packets of Creamer Whitener (U.K.)
>4 x Packets of White Sugar (U.K.)
>2 x Typhoo Teabags 2g (U.K.)
>2 x Kenco Coffee Packets (U.K.)
>Pack of 6 Water Purifying Tablets (U.K.)
>Packet of Boiled Sweets 50g (Poland)
>3 x Packets of Dental Chewing Gum (Denmark)
>Small Bottle of Tabasco Green Sauce (U.S.A.)
>2 Packets Antiseptic Wipes (U.K.)
>Packet of Matches (U.K.)
>Plastic Spoon (U.K.)

The use envisaged for the pack is for a light breakfast and lunch, with an evening main meal and snacks available at other times.

The contents of the Meal Pouches and the Fruit Puree would of course vary in different packs.

Sources & Select Bibliography

There have been only two works written, neither officially published, that are specifically about food for the British soldier. Much, however, appears in histories of military transport and supply and still more often simply a sentence or two scattered around regimental and campaign histories. I have used, and I hope in this bibliography suitably acknowledged, material they contain.

The two unpublished works, a copy of each of which is available for study and photocopying at the Museum of the Royal Logistic Corps at Deepcut in Surrey are "The Story of the Army Catering Corps" edited by Howard N. Cole, and the more succinct booklet, "The Soldiers' Food", by Major F.A. Gaunt and Captain C.A. Jones. Both works contain chronological period or campaign chapters from early days to the late 20th Century. The Army Catering Corps was later merged into the new Royal Logistic Corps.

The means by which food reached the front-line soldier in the 20th Century ranged from mule, horse or pony, oxen, camel, reindeer, even elephant, to human porters and on to motor vehicles, aircraft and helicopters. The four key works are John Fortescue, *The Royal Army Service Corps, Vol. 1* and Colonel R.H. Beadon, *The Royal Army Service Corps, Vol. 2,* both Cambridge University Press, 1930 and 1931 respectively, and *The Story of the Royal Army Service Corps 1939-1945,* G. Bell, (n.d.), together with John Sutton, *Wait For the Waggons, The Story of the Royal Corps of Transport and its Predecessors,* Leo Cooper, 1998. Copies of these, and all the further works listed in the period chapters, are all held in the Library of the Royal Military Academy Sandhurst, Camberley. The publishers and dates cited are those on the Sandhurst Library copies, a number have been reprinted and published elsewhere.

Chapter 1

Both general and Regimental histories provide useful detail, the most rewarding are:

W.J.P. Aggett, *The Bloody Eleventh, History of the Devonshire Regiment, Vol. II 1815-1914,* Devonshire & Dorset Regiment, (1995)
J.S.G. Blair, *Centenary History of the Royal Army Medical Corps 1898-1948,* Lynx, (2001). This work notes the origin of the word Scoff.
Lieut-Colonel A.D. Greenhill Gardyne, *The Life of a Regiment, Volume III 1898-1914. The History of the Gordon Highlanders during and after the Boer War,* Leo Cooper (1972), which gives detail about the siege of Ladysmith.
C.B. Knight, *Historical Records of The Buffs (Royal East Kent Regiment), 3rd Foot 1814-1914,* Medici Society, (1951).
Thomas Pakenham, *The Boer War,* Weidenfeld, (1979).
Geoffrey Powell, *Buller, A Scapegoat?,* Pen & Sword Books, (1994), and *The History of the Green Howards,* Arms and Armour, (1992)
Nicholas Riall, *The Letters, Diaries and Photographs of Malcolm Riall from the War in South Africa 1899-1902,* Brassey's, (1999)
John Selby, *The Boer War,* Barker, (1969), a particularly well-written overview
Lieutenant Colonel J. Watkins-Yardley, *With the Iniskilling Dragoons. The Record of a Cavalry Regiment during the Boer War, 1899-1902,* Naval & Military Press, (2006) (originally published Longmans, Green & Co., 1902).

Chapter 2

Many works concerning the Western Front exist. These noted here proved to be the most useful:

Alastair Campbell of Airds, *Argyll and Sutherland Highlanders,* History Press (2005)
John Baynes, *Morale: a Study of Men and Courage,* Pen & Sword (1987)
Stephen Bull, *Trench, A History of Trench Warfare,* Osprey, (2010)
Martin Gilbert, *First World War,* Phoenix, (2008)
R.H. Haig and R.W. Turner, *The Battle of the Somme 1916, The Experience of the 13th (Service) Battalion of the York and Lancaster Regiment,* Sheffield City

Polytechnic, Department of Political Studies, (1983), a fine Kitchener Army soldier's account.

Richard Holmes, *Tommy*, Harper Collins, (2005), a great work encompassing all features of a Western Front soldier's life.

Steve Hurst, *The Public Schools Battalion in the Great War*, Pen & Sword, (2007)

Peter H. Liddle, *The British Soldier on the Somme, 1916*, Strategic and Combat Studies Institute, Staff College, (1996)

Robin Neilland, *The Old Contemptibles, the British Expeditionary Force, 1914*, John Murray, (2004). The very few comments that my late father, an 'Old Contemptible', permitted himself to make corroborate this narrative.

A. Pawn, *Pawns in the Retreat from Mons*, Isle of Wight Country Press, (1916)

Denis Winter, *Death's Men, Soldiers at the Great War*, Penguin, (1979)

Chapter 3

Feeding soldiers in more distant campaigns before the age of air transport raised formidable problems.

Dardanelles

Henry Hanna, *The Pals at Suvla Bay: Being the Record of D Company, the 7th Battalion The Royal Dublin Fusiliers*, Ponsonby, (1916)

Robert Rhodes James, *Gallipoli*, Batsford, (1916)

Mesopotamia (Iraq)

Russell Braddon, *The Siege*, Jonathon Cape, (1969)

Captain J.E.H. Neville, *History of the 43rd and 52nd Light Infantry in the Great War, 1914-1919*, Gale & Polden (1938)

F. Loraine Petrie, *History of the Norfolk Regiment 2006: 4th August 1914 to 31st December 1918*, Jarrold, (n.d.)

Sinai, Palestine Syria

E.W. Gladstone, *The Shropshire Yeomanry*, Whitethorne, (1953)

Edward C. Woodland, *Camp and Combat on the Sinai and Palestine Front*, Palgrave Macmillan (2012)

David Woodward, *Forgotten Soldiers of the First World War*, Tempus, (2006)

Salonika and Macedonia

Harold Lake, *In Salonika with Our Army*, Melrose, n.d.
Charles Packer, *Return to Salonika*, Cassell, (1964).
Alan Wakefield and Simon Moody, *Under the Devil's Eye*, Sutton, (2004)
Personal recollections passed on from this author's late father who served in the campaign also provided detail.

Italy

Martin Hardy and Warner Allen, *Our Italian Front*, A.C. Black, (1920)
Captain J.E.H. Neville, *History of the 43rd and 52nd Light Infantry in the Great War, 1914-1919*, Gale & Polden (1938)
John Wilks and Eileen Wilks, *The British Army in Italy, 1917-1918*, Leo Cooper (1998)

Russia

Beadon, *Royal Army Service Corps Vol. 2*, is the only work that provides a satisfactory account of the logistic problems. The work includes interesting pictures of reindeer transport.

Chapter 4

The Army was engaged in a number of small-scale campaigns in the inter-war years, some with difficulties in food supply and transport. Also, though not necessarily directed towards the military, academic research into diet was taking place.

Anthony Clayton, *The British Empire as a Superpower, 1918-1939*, University of Georgia and Macmillan, (1986)
Lizzie Collingham, *The Taste of War, World War Two and the Battle for Food*, Allen Lane, (2011). A seminal study of great importance
Charles Gwynne, *Imperial Policing*, Macmillan, (1934)
J.P. Riley, *From Pole to Pole*, Bluntisham Books, (1989)

Chapter 5

Anon, *Infantry Officer, A Personal Record, Norway and France, 1940,* Batsford, (1943)
Gregory Blaxland, *Destination Dunkirk,* William Kimber, (1973)
Joseph Kynock, *Norway 1940, the Forgotten Fiasco,* Crowood, (2002)
Peter Hadley, *Third Class to Dunkirk,* Hollis And Carter, (1944)
Robert Jackson, *Dunkirk, The British Evacuation 1940,* Arthur Barker, (1976)
Hugh Sebag-Montefiore, *Dunkirk, Fight to the Last Man,* Penguin, (2007)

Malta

Aggett, *Bloody Eleventh,* notes the food difficulties of a British battalion during the siege of Malta

North Africa

A number of works tell of the supply problems of fast moving forward armour in the three successive campaigns of Generals Wavell, Auchinleck and Montgomery.
Major W.R. Beddington, *A History of the Queen's Bays, 1929-1945,* Warren (1954)
Dudley Clarke, *Eleventh at War,* Michael Joseph, (1952). Eleventh refers to the Eleventh Hussars
Driver Robert John Crawford, *I Was an Eighth Army Soldier,* Victor Gollancz, (1944)
Jonathan Fennell, *Combat and Morale in the North African Campaign,* Cambridge University Press, (2011)
Adrian Gilbert, *The Imperial War Museum Book of the Desert War,* Sidgwick & Jackson (1992)
A, Heckstall Smith, *Tobruk,* Anthony Blond, (1959)
Major Kenneth Macksey and Richard Hull, *A History of the Royal Armoured Corps 1914-1975,* Newtown (1983)
Major Tony Mellor, *Machine Gunner,* Hutchinson, (1948)
William Moore, *Panzer Bait, With the 3rd Royal Tank Regiment, 19401944,* Pen & Sword (1991)
J.P.H. Pitt-Rivers, *The Story of the Royal Dragoons,* Clowes, (1956)

East Africa

A household name Richard Dimbleby, *The Frontiers are Green*, Hodder & Stoughton, (1944) describes the hazards of food supply in Eritrea during the Italian East Africa campaign.

Chapter 6

Italy

Alex Bowlby, *Recollections of Rifleman Bowlby*, Leo Cooper, (1969)
Philip Brutton, *An Ensign in Italy*, Pen & Sword, (1992)
Lieutenant-Colonel R.M.P. Carver, *Second to None, The Royal Scots Greys, 1919-1945*, Printed for the Regt. by McCorquodale, (1954)
Lieutenant-Colonel H.D. Chaplin, *The Queen's Own Royal West Kent Regiment, 1920-1950*, Michael Joseph, (1954)
Lloyd Clark, *Anzio*, Headline (2007)
Wilf Goldstein, *Farewell Screw Gun*, Book Guild, (1986)
Fred Madjalany, *The Monastery*, John Lane (1945)
Raleigh Trevelyan, *The Fortress*, Collins, (1956)

North-West Europe

This section covers operations from Normandy to the end of the European War.
Alan Borthwick, *Battalion*, Baton Wicks, (1994) of especial interest in the rations for soldiers landing in France on D-Day
Sydney Jary, *18 Platoon*, Jary, (1998)
Ralph Thompson, *The 15th/19th King's Royal Hussars, A Pictorial History*, Quoin, (1989)
Peter White, *With the Jocks, A Soldier's Struggle for Europe, 1944-45*, History Press (2002)

Malaya

Only the full account in Beadon, *Royal Army Service Corps Vol. 2* provides logistic detail of this unfortunate campaign.

Madagascar

Jonathon Riley, *The Life and Campaigns of General Hughie Stockwell*, Pen & Sword Military, (2006) records a campaign, Madagascar, in 1942, where food was often abundant. The reverse was to be the case in Burma.

Burma

Louis Allen, *Burma, The Longest War 1941-45*, Phoenix, (1998)

Lieutenant-Colonel J.J. Burke-Gaffney, *The Story of the King's Regiment, 1914-1945*, Sharpe and Kellet, (1954)

Michael Calvert, *Chindits, Long Range Penetration*, Pan, (1958)

Raymond Cooper, *B Company*, Dobson Books (1979)

Colonel J.M. Cowper, *The King's Own, the Story of a Royal Regiment, III 1914-1950*, Gale and Polden, (1957)

Stuart Eastwood, *Lions of England, A Pictorial History of the King's Own Royal Regiment (Lancaster), 1680-1980*, Silver Link, (1991)

Geoffrey Evans and Antony Brett-James, *Imphal: A Flower on Lofty Heights*, Macmillan, (1962)

George MacDonald Fraser, *Quartered Safe Out Here*, Harvill, (1993)

Ian Latimer, *Burma, The Forgotten War*, John Murray, (2005)

John Masters, *The Road Past Mandalay*, Michael Joseph, (1961), a classic

Trevor Royle, *Orde Wingate Irregular Soldier*, Weidenfeld & Nicolson (1995). Of the many books on this military eccentric this work is recommended.

Lowell Thomas, *Back to Mandalay*, Frederick Miller, (1972)

Julian Thompson, *The Imperial War Museum Book of the War in Burma, 1942-45*, Sidgwick & Jackson, (2002), an immensely useful source book

O.G.W. White, *Straight On For Tokyo*, Gale & Polden, (1948), a particularly good account of a British battalion in the campaign

Rachel S. Johnstone, "Operational Rations and Anglo-American Long-Range Infantry in Burma 1942-1944, a Sub-Cultural Study of Combat Feeding" D. Phil thesis, Oxford University, 2000. A copy of this work can be found at the Royal Logistic Corps Museum, Deepcut.

Chapter 7

Palestine

Max Arthur, *Men of the Red Beret, Airborne Forces 1940-1990*, Hutchinson, (1990)
Geoffrey Blaxland,. *The Regiments Depart*, William Kimber, (1971)
Oliver Lindsay, *Once a Grenadier*, Pen & Sword (1996)

Malaya

C. Bannister, *An Inch of Bravery, 3 R.A.R. in the Malayan Emergency 1957-59*, Directorate of Army Public Affairs, Canberra, (1994)
Malcolm K. Johnson, *Yield to None, The History of the King's Own Yorkshire Light Infantry, 1945-1968*, Propagator Press, (2005)
Frank Kitson, *Bunch of Five*, Faber (2010)
Richard Miers, *Shoot to Kill*, Faber, (1959)
A. Walker and Others, *A County Regiment, The 1st Battalions The Queen's Own Royal West Kent Regiment, Malaya, 1951-54*, published by the Regiment. This work contains excellent detail on food.
J.N.P. Watson, *The Story of the Blues and Royals*, Pen & Sword (1993)

Kenya

Aggett, *Bloody Eleventh, Volume III, 1914-69*
Fred Madjalany, *State of Emergency*, Longman, (1962)

Cyprus

Campbell of Airds, *Argyll and Sutherland Highlanders*
Johnson, *Yield to None*

Aden

Brigadier Frank Steer, *To the Warrior His Arms*, Leo Cooper (2005)
Jonathan Walker, *Aden Insurgency, The Savage War in South Arabia 1962-67*, History Press (2004)

Korea

Soldiers fed on American as well as British rations…
Brigadier C.N. Barclay, *The First Commonwealth Division*, Gale & Polden, (1954)
Tom Carew, *Korea, The Commonwealth at War*, Cassell, (1967) and
The Glorious Glosters, Leo Cooper (1970)
René Cutforth, *Korean Reporter*, Allan Wingate (1952)
Brigadier B.A.H. Parritt, *Chinese Hordes and Human Waves*, Pen & Sword Military, (2011)
David R Orr and David Truesdale, *A New Battlefield: The Royal Ulster Rifles in Korea 1950-51*, Helion (2011)
Julian Tunstall, *I Fought in Korea*, Lawrence & Wishart (1953)
D.E. Whatmore, *One Road to Imjin*, Dew Line Publications, (1997)
A copy of a valuable unpublished paper "Haute Cuisine in the Land of Morning Calm, 1955" was sent to me by its author, Lieutenant-Colonel P.E. Duffield.

Suez

Riley, *General Hughie Stockwell*,
Julian Thompson, *Ready for Anything, The Parachute Regiment at War, 1940-1982*, Weidenfeld & Nicolson, (1989)

Borneo

A very instructive campaign. Food was in good supply, conditions for its consumption were often very difficult.
Nick van der Bijl, *Confrontation, the War in Indonesia 1962-1966*, Pen & Sword (2007)
Mike Kelly, *The Last Conflict, The Durham Light Infantry, Borneo, 1966*, Broadcast Books (2004)
James Ladd, *Royal Marine Commando*, Littlehampton Book Services, (1985)
Thompson, *Ready for Anything*

Chapter 8

Northern Ireland

Oliver Lindsay, *Once a Grenadier,* Pen & Sword, (1996)
Major-General L.T.H. Phelps, *A History of the Royal Army Ordnance Corps, 1945-82,* Royal Army Ordnance Corps, (1991) is of particular interest on local issues of supply in Northern Ireland. This author was also helped by notes from Julian James based on his experiences.

Falkland Islands

The Falkland War's problems of distance and of long marches before battle make most interesting reading, including:
Major-General John Frost, *2 Para Falklands, The Battalion at War,* Buchan & Enright (1984)
Murray Naylor, *Among Friends, The Scots Guards, 1956-1993,* Pen & Sword, (1995)
Thompson, *Ready for Anything,* (1989)
Hew Pike, *From the Front Line. Family Letters and Diaries: 1914 to the Falklands and Afghanistan,* Pen & Sword, (2008) and a manuscript "Falklands Catering Section War Diary" (copy held in the Royal Logistics Corps Museum, Deepcut). The author was greatly helped by the opportunity of a discussion with Lieutenant-General Sir Hew Pike and an informative letter from Julian James, again based on personal experience.

First Gulf War

General Sir Peter de la Billière, *Storm Command,* HarperCollins, (2008)
Major-General Patrick Cordingley, *In the Eye of the Storm,* Hodder and Stoughton, (1996)
Andrew Gillespie, *Desert Fire, The Story of a Gulf War Gunner,* Pen & Sword, (2001)

Bosnia-Herzegovina

Michael Glover and Jonathon Riley, '*The Astonishing Infantry*', *The History of the Royal Welch Fusiliers, 1689-2000,* Pen & Sword (2007)
Les Howard, *Winter Warriors, Across Bosnia With the P.B.I,* Book Guild (2006)
David Langley, *White Dragon,* Royal Welch Fusiliers (1997)

Rupert Wolfe-Murray, Ed., *IFOR on IFOR, NATO Peacekeepers in Bosnia-Herzegovina,* Connect, (1906).

The author also received very interesting recollections from Lieutenant-General Jonathon Riley for which he is especially grateful.

<u>Second Gulf War</u>

Richard Holmes, *Dusty Warrior, Modern Soldiers at War,* Harper Collins (2007)
Sgt. Dan Mills, *Sniper One,* Penguin, (2008)
Mark Nicol, *Condor Blues, British Soldiers at War,* Mainstream Publishing, (2007)

<u>Afghanistan</u>

A conflict unfinished at the time of writing, but early books occasionally touch on food.

Patrick Bishop, *3 Para, Afghanistan Summer 2006, This is War,* Harper Collins (2007), war still being ongoing.
Toby Harnden, *Dead Men Risen,* Quercus (2011)
Patrick Hennessey, *The Junior Officers' Reading Club,* London, Allen Lane, (2009)
Pike, *From the Front Line,*
An article, "Pressure Cookers" in *EQPD,* issue of April 2011, is also of interest. A relative currently serving in Afghanistan not only provided most useful information but also a soldier's daily ration box.

There is a copy of the "Warrant for establishing a more regular system in the issue of Rations of Provisions to Her Majesty's Forces at Foreign Stations, 1816" in the Royal Logistic Corps Museum, Deepcut.

Index

1st Army, ii, 57
1st Princess of Wales' Royal
    Regiment, 92
1st Queen's Royal Regiment, 74
1st Royal Welch Fusiliers, 90
5th Army, 27
8th Army, *see* Eighth Army
27th Brigade, 78
29 Brigade, 79

Aberdares, 74
Aden, 70, 75, 76, 108
Afghan Army, 93
Afghanistan, iii-iv, ix, xi, 83, 93-94,
    96-97, 99, 110-111
Africa, iv, viii, 15-16, 29, 48-49, 56,
    57, 60, 102, 105, 106
Afrika Korps, 47, 50, 53, 56
Al Amrah, 92
Aldershot, viii, 20, 21, 36, 41, 43-44,
    48
'Aldershot Kitchen', 20
Alexandria, 50, 53-54
Algeria, ii, 56-57
Allenby, General Sir Edmund, 34
Al Qaeda, 93

American Meals Ready to Eat, 87
Antarctic, 39, 42
Anzio, ii, viii, 58-59, 106
Arakan, 65-66
Archangel, 38
Argyll and Sutherland
    Highlanders, 78, 102, 108
Army Catering Corps, vi, ix, 45, 61,
    70, 73, 101
Army of the Nile, 50
Arnhem, 62
Auchinleck, General Sir Claude, 50

Baghdad, 32, 34, 40
B.A.O.R., 70
Basra, 91-93
Bastion, Camp, 93, 95-96
Belgium, 46, 62
'Benghazi Burner', x, 50-51, 63, 79,
    90
Bluff Cove, 85
Boer War, ii-iii, vii, viii-ix, 13-14,
    16-20, 22-23, 97, 102
Borneo, ii, 70, 81-83, 109
Bosnia-Herzegovina, iii, ix, 14, 89,
    110, 111

Index   113

Boyd Orr, Sir John, 42
'The Buffs' (Royal East Kent
    Regiment), 18, 102
Buller, Sir Redvers, 18-19, 102
Burma, ii, 40, 55, 65-66, 69, 71, 107
Byford, Richard, 41

Caen, 62
Calabria, 58-59
Chindits, ii, viii, 66, 68-69
Chinook, 95
Coldstream Guards, 95
Constantinople, 30
Cordingley, Brigadier, 88, 110
Crete, 53
Cyprus, 35, 70, 74, 108
Cyrenaica, 50

Deepcut, iii, ix, 101, 107, 110-111
Devonshire Regiment, 18-19, 48, 102
Diego Suarez, 64
Dunkirk, 46-47, 105

East Africa, 29, 106
Egypt, 15, 29, 34-35, 47-50, 75, 80
Eighth Army, 50, 56-57, 105
El Alamein, 50, 53
Eritrea, 53, 106
Ethiopia, 53

Falklands War, iii, vi, 85, 90, 110
First Fusiliers Battle Group, 92
Forest Emergency regiments, 74

Forward Locality Bases, 81-82
Forward Observation Base, 96
Forward Operation Bases, 93
France, iv, viii, 22, 28, 38, 42-44, 46, 62, 64, 80, 105, 106

Gallipoli, 29-31, 103
German East Africa, 29
Gloucestershire Regiment, viii, xii, 24, 77, 79-80, 109
Goose Green, 85-86
Gorazde, iii, 89-91
Gordon Highlanders, 19, 102
Gort, Lord, 46, 48
Greece, 36, 50, 53
Green Howards (Alexandra, Princess
    of Wales's Own Yorkshire
    Regiment), viii, 18, 58, 102
Guards, viii, 81, 84-87, 90, 95, 110
Guards Parachute Company, 81
Gurkhas, 84

Helmand, ii, iii, 93
Holland, 62-63
Hore-Belisha, Leslie, 41

Imjin River, 80, 109
Imphal, 66-67, 107
India, ii, 15, 19, 29, 32-34, 40, 46, 53, 59-60, 64-66
Indian Army, 32, 53
Indonesia, 81-82, 109
Indonesian Army, 81
Intelligence Corps, iv, 86

Iraq, ii, iii, ix, 32, 40, 83, 87, 91-93, 103
Israel, 71, 80
Italy, 14, 29, 38, 55, 57-58, 104, 106

Japan, 55, 64-65

Kabul, 93
Kenya, iv, 29, 70, 74, 108
Kenya (Mount), 74
Kenya Police Reserve Air Wing, 74
King's Own Royal Regiment (Lancaster), 16, 17, 24, 61, 66, 68, 107
Kohima, 66-67
Korean War, ii, 70, 76, 80, 90
Kosovo, ix, 36
Kut El Amara, ii, 32-33, 40, 51
Kuwait, 87

Ladysmith, ii, 19, 51, 102
Libya, ii, viii, 48, 50, 52
Longdon, 85

Macedonia, 29, 36-37, 104
'Maconochie', 17, 24, 31, 38, 59
Madagascar, 55, 64, 107
Maidstone, 83-84
Malaya, viii, 55, 64, 70-72, 74, 81, 106, 108
Malta, viii, 47-48, 57, 105
Marne, 22, 27
Mau Mau, 74
Mersa Matruh, 53

Mesopotamia, 32, 35, 103
Mexeflotes, 86
Middle East, 46, 48-49, 53-54
Middlesex Regiment, 78
Mons, ii, 26, 103
Monte Cassino, ii, 60
Montgomery, General Sir Bernard, 50
Morocco, 56
MRE, viii, 87-88, 92
Murmansk, 38

NAAFI, 41, 45, 73, 80
Nairobi, 74
Narvik, 44
NATO, 70, 89-90, 93, 111
New Zealand, 30, 69, 99
Normandy, ii, 61, 63, 106
North Africa, viii, 48-49, 56-57, 105
Northern Ireland, iii, 83, 110, 118
Norway, 43, 55, 100, 105

Ottoman Empire, 30, 36

Palestine, viii, 29, 34-35, 70-71, 103, 108
Paphos, 74
Parachute Regiment, vi, viii, xii, 57, 82, 84-86, 93, 109
Pearl Harbor, 64
Port Said, 80
Port Stanley, 86

Radfan, 75

Rangoon, 66
Rhine River, 63, 70
Riley, Quintin, 42, 55
Roberts, General Lord, 18
Rome, 58, 60
Rommel, General Erwin, ii, 50, 53
Royal Air Force, 27, 53, 74
Royal Army Service Corps, 15, 34, 101, 104, 106
Royal British Legion, 88
Royal Dublin Fusiliers, 18, 103
Royal Engineers, 88
Royal Flying Corps, 33-34
Royal Logistic Corps Museum, iii, xii, 107, 111
Royal Marines, 76, 80, 84
Royal Military Academy Sandhurst, iii-iv, ix, xii, 101
Royal Navy, 47, 51, 54, 64, 76, 83-84
Royal Ulster Rifles, 78, 109, 118
Royal Welch Fusiliers, 89-90, 110
Royal West Kent Regiment, 73, 106, 108

Saddam Hussein, 91
Salerno, ii, 58, 59
Salmon, Sir Isidore, 41
Salonika, viii, 36-37, 104
Scots Guards, 85-86, 110
Senior Catering Officer Field Force, iii, ix, 15
Seoul, 76-77
Serbia, 36
Sicily, 55, 57
Shackleton, Sir Ernest, 39
Somme, 21-22, 26, 102, 103

Southern Arabia, 75
South Korea, 76-77
Spion Kop, 18
Sudan, 35, 50, 53
Suez Canal, 34, 70, 80, 109
Suvla Bay, 31-32, 103
Syria, 29, 34, 53, 103

Taliban, 93-95
Tanzania, 29
Templer, General, Sir Gerald, 71
Territorial Army, iv, viii, 41, 43
Tigris, 32-34
Tobruk, 50-52, 105
Townshend, General Sir Charles Vere Ferrers, 32
Troodos, 74-75
Tumbledown (Mount), 85-86
Tunisia, ii, 55-57
Turkey, 30

Vichy France, 53, 64

Wavell, General Sir Archibald, 50
Welsh Guards, 90
Wingate, Brigadier Orde, 68, 107, 109
Women's Army Auxiliary Corps, 26

Yemen, 75
Ypres, 21-22, 26, 27
Yugoslavia, 83, 89